Prudence Hatchett

Evolutionary Resilience

Conquering the Emotional Intrusions of Anxiety, Depression, & Trauma

ISBN: 978-1-966798-60-6

Table of Contents

Introduction

Resilience is often misunderstood. People think it's about gritting your teeth, pushing through, and pretending everything is fine. But true resilience isn't about suffering in silence, it's about **learning how to rise, heal, and evolve.** For years, I witnessed people wrestling with anxiety, depression, and trauma, believing they were failing rather than naturally responding to life's hardships. We don't wake up one day *choosing* to feel anxious or overwhelmed. These emotions don't appear out of thin air. They are deeply woven into how we view ourselves, how we process the world, and even how our bodies function on a physiological level.

Think about it: If you had a headache, you wouldn't blame yourself for it. You'd take care of your body, maybe drink some water, get some rest, or take medicine. But when we feel anxious, sad, or emotionally exhausted, we tend to do the opposite, we blame ourselves, isolate, and believe we are somehow broken or somewhat deserve to feel this way. We may even continue to try to pour from an empty cup or operate from an empty soul.

As someone who has spent close to two decades working at the intersection of mental health, education, and personal development, I bring a deeply rooted and well-rounded perspective to the topic of resilience. My journey as a **licensed counselor, certified coach, educator, business owner, author,** and **speaker** has allowed me to guide thousands of individuals through some of the most difficult emotional stages of their lives. I've worked in schools, clinical settings, boardrooms, and community spaces, always with the same mission, to help people transform pain into power and fear into growth. Through years of hands-on experience, I've witnessed how real-life struggles like anxiety, depression, trauma, and emotional setbacks can feel impossible to navigate, until someone gives you the tools, language, and encouragement to take your healing seriously. That's what I've dedicated my life to doing. Resilience isn't just something I teach, **it's something I live, model, and help others embody every day.**

That's why I wrote this book.

This book is your roadmap to healing the emotional intrusions caused by anxiety, depression, and trauma. Not through forced positivity or unrealistic self-help mantras, but through **real, science-backed strategies** that will help you take control of your emotional and physical well-being. We will explore:

- How intrusive thoughts and negative emotional patterns take root and how to rewrite them
- The connection between mental health and physical health, including nutrition, hormones, and chronic stress
- How to create an internal safety zone where self-trust and emotional security replace self-doubt and fear
- Why resilience is not just about surviving but about thriving

I chose the term **"emotional intrusions"** because it captures the experience of those persistent, often unwanted thoughts and feelings that seem to hijack our emotional space without warning. These intrusions disrupt our inner peace, distort our self-perception, and interfere with our ability to grow emotionally. They can stem from anxiety, depression, trauma, or even past conditioning and often feel so familiar that we begin to mistake them for truth. By naming them as *intrusions*, I wanted to highlight that these emotional patterns are not a reflection of who we are at our core, but rather disruptions to our natural development and mental clarity. Recognizing them as intrusions gives us the power to pause, examine them with compassion, and begin the process of reclaiming our emotional space.

Evolutionary Resilience is about **understanding your mind and body so you can stop fighting yourself and start working with yourself.** Anxiety, depression, and trauma don't just affect your thoughts; they affect your nervous system, your energy levels, your decision-making, and even your physical health. If you've ever struggled with exhaustion, brain fog, or a body that feels constantly tense, know that your emotional struggles are real experiences that should not be ignored.

You are not broken. You do not have to stay stuck. Healing is not about fixing yourself; it's about reclaiming yourself.

Are you ready to take back your mind, your body, and your spirit? Let's begin.

With Gratitude,
Prudence Hatchett
PH Counseling, LLC & Learn with Prudence
www.phcounseling.org

I was inspired to write a book about resilience because I wanted to help people strengthen their mental abilities to navigate and withstand emotional intrusions. What are emotional intrusions? I define emotional intrusions as disruptions that hinder our emotional development and growth. This disruption can include, but not limited to trauma, negative mindset, abuse, childhood abuse, or toxic relationships. I purposefully designed this book to include psychoeducation, helpful insights, and strategies that will help explain the importance of resilience and managing difficult emotions, or as I would call them, emotional intrusions.

In general, these emotional intrusions can be categorized into three main areas: anxiety, depression, and trauma. Anxiety often manifests as persistent worry, fear, or overthinking, making it difficult to stay present and emotionally balanced. Depression can create feelings of hopelessness, low energy, and emotional numbness, hindering personal growth and resilience. Trauma, whether from past experiences or ongoing stress, can leave deep emotional wounds that interfere with one's ability to process emotions and build healthy coping mechanisms. Understanding these categories helps in recognizing and addressing the emotional barriers that may be limiting growth and well-being.

As you noticed, the title includes the term, *evolutionary,* because I wanted to signal to you (the reader) that this journey is about growth, transformation, and gaining new perspectives. My goal was to prepare you for insights that may challenge conventional thinking, possibly confirm internal thoughts, encourage personal development, and inspire a deeper understanding of resilience. Just as evolution is a process of adaptation and progress, the insights in this book are meant to help readers evolve emotionally and mentally, equipping them with the tools to navigate life's challenges with greater strength and awareness.

Welcome to Evolutionary Resilience: Conquering the emotional intrusions of Anxiety, Depression, and Trauma.

What should I do after crying all night
Laying in tears of sorrow
Until the birth of daylight

Who shall I talk to after the anger outburst
Throwing a tantrum
Making myself feel worse

I try to look within to see the best in myself
Mentally scanning from head to toe
While putting my feelings on a shelf

I suppose I should wear a mask
Tiptoeing around the attitude of others
Feeling trapped like liquor in a flask

Who should I run to when deep in despair
Feeling unloved and chafed
Unknown like who, what, and where

But I must pull myself up by the bootstraps
Dust off my shirt and pants
Love my life like before all the emotional gaps

I will walk strong again and not bend
One step at a time
All before the day's end

It's the strength in my bones
It's the twinkle in my eyes
I'm coming alive like a blossomed cherry
I feel evolutionary

-Prudence Hatchett

CHAPTER 1

What is Resilience?

The primary purpose of resilience and emotional intelligence is to help us navigate life's ups and downs with stability, confidence, and adaptability. Resilience allows us to recover from setbacks, handle stress, and keep striving toward our goals, while emotional intelligence helps us understand, regulate, and express our emotions effectively. Without these skills, we may struggle with anxiety, frustration, or burnout, finding it difficult to cope with challenges or maintain healthy relationships. Poor emotional management can lead to impulsive reactions, miscommunication, and unnecessary conflicts, while a lack of resilience can make setbacks feel overwhelming, causing us to give up too easily. Developing these skills is crucial for personal growth, well-being, and overall success in life.

Resilience is more than just surviving or pushing through difficult times. Simply getting through can mean numbing the pain with distractions, substances, or unhealthy habits—just existing rather than truly healing. But real resilience is about how you get through challenges. It means navigating hardships in a way that is emotionally safe and secure, treating your mind and body with kindness, and choosing coping mechanisms that promote healing rather than harm. True resilience isn't about avoiding pain. It's about facing it with self-compassion, emotional awareness, and the strength to grow from adversity rather than being consumed by it.

We respond to life's stressors based on what we know at the moment. Meaning, instead of emotional healing, we will likely experience emotional survival. During the process of emotional healing, we process events that have caused pain or struggle, seeking support such as counseling or coaching, creating a universal self-help plan, and maybe even working towards improving our physical health. During the emotional survival phase, we are likely to suppress emotions, attempting to forget the past or trauma, using substances, or using anger outburst as the main emotional outlet. Unfortunately, this phase can last as long as a lifetime for some people, mainly because they do not know that they can feel better. They have accepted their fate to just try to survive one day at a time.

This book is not about placing blame or judgment on anyone, especially not yourself. Growth begins with self-compassion, not self-criticism. The reality is, there are things we simply haven't learned yet, and that's okay. Emotional regulation, for example, can feel like an unattainable or even unrealistic goal for some. It might seem "fake" or forced, making it difficult to trust as a real solution. Others may struggle with it because they don't trust the source of the information or have never seen healthy emotional regulation modeled in their own lives. Whatever the reason, this book is here to bridge that gap, to break down emotional resilience into approachable, practical steps and show that it is possible to navigate emotions in a way that feels natural, empowering, and sustainable.

Emotional survival is a state of constantly reacting rather than responding. It means operating on autopilot, driven by stress, fear, or past wounds, rather than intentional thought or self-awareness. When we are in emotional survival mode, our nervous system is often in a heightened state—quick to anger, easily overwhelmed, or prone to shutting down. Instead of processing emotions in a healthy way, we may lash out, withdraw, or rely on unhealthy coping mechanisms just to get through the moment. True emotional resilience, on the other hand, allows us to pause, assess, and respond with clarity and self-compassion, rather than being controlled by knee-jerk reactions. Moving from emotional survival to emotional resilience is about shifting from just getting through life's challenges to growing through them.

My main goal for teaching about resilience is to move from reactionary responses to emotional prevention. Being too reactive will keep you in a survival state of mind, where emotions dictate your actions without you having emotional control. In this state, your nervous system is constantly on high alert, making it difficult to think clearly, regulate emotions, or make thoughtful decisions. Instead of responding with intention, you may find yourself snapping in anger, shutting down emotionally, or feeling overwhelmed by even small stressors. This cycle can create a sense of powerlessness, reinforcing the idea that emotions control you rather than the other way around. True emotional growth comes from breaking this pattern, learning to pause, process, and respond in a way that aligns with your values rather than reacting out of habit or fear.

Examples of reactionary responses:

1. Angry outburst with a friend because there was miscommunication about the plans for the evening.
2. Being physically abusive to your partner because they make you angry.
3. Using emotionally damaging words with your child because you are tired from working long hours.
4. Keying your spouse's car because you caught them cheating.
5. Jumping over the check-out counter because you thought you were being overcharged.

Emotional healing is closely linked to preventative measures because true healing isn't just about recovering from past wounds, it's also about building the tools to protect yourself from future emotional harm. Just as physical health relies on both treatment and prevention, emotional well-being depends on proactive habits that strengthen resilience, self-awareness, and emotional regulation. This means setting healthy boundaries, recognizing emotional triggers, practicing self-care, and developing coping mechanisms that promote long-term stability. By taking preventative steps, you create a strong foundation that reduces the impact of stress, anxiety, and emotional setbacks, allowing you to navigate life with greater confidence and emotional security. Healing isn't just about looking back, it's also about moving forward with the tools to protect your peace. Prevention can help us feel like we are in control of our emotions because we have a plan of action, when we are experiencing these strong emotions.

Examples of emotion healing responses:

(refer to the examples of reactionary responses above)

1. Make an intentional decision to calmly contact your friend and communicate about the misunderstanding, which will likely lead to a new plan for the evening.
2. Express your discontentment and anger using your words. The more direct and concise you are, the more you are likely to be understood. [Side note: physical abuse is never the answer to solve any problem].
3. Take deep breaths before responding to your child. This create time and space for you to calmly respond, instead of directing your anger at the child (who doesn't deserve it).

Please listen to me, resilience nor healing means ignoring or forgetting the past. In fact, attempting to forget can cause more harm because forgetting is linked to suppression. Suppression can happen consciously (intentionally) by attempting to avoid negative thoughts, ignore uncomfortable feelings, or pretending that certain events did not happen. Again, I understand that we will react using the routine behavior that we have at the current moment. However, eventually growth is a personal decision and a solo journey that you must decide to partake in if you want your life and mental health to improve. And it's a decision that you must make every day.

Suppression may also happen through subconscious activity (unintentional). This may happen when the brain is attempting to protect you from a harmful experience. You may remember these events later in life through dreams or flashbacks, uncovering bits and pieces of the suppressed memory at a time. When you start to remember these bits and pieces, the information in your subconscious brain is transferring the information to your conscious brain making you aware of your memories. Some people may think that forgetting harmful experiences is better for them, or somehow less painful. But forgetting or suppression is an indicator of a cognitive deficit, because our brain is designed to remember information. The brain's functions include assisting us in problem-solving, facilitating interactions with others, ensuring our survival in various environments, and supporting our developmental learning and growth. So, when your brain is "remembering" information, that is the brain operating at its functional level. This is your brain speaking to you. When your brain speaks, it's trying to teach you something.

In essence, true and long-lasting resilience includes:

1. Recognizing your feelings and thoughts (this will lead to what is blocking your ability to be resilient).
2. Making an intentional decision that you want to change your reactions.
3. Seeking the support of a therapist.
4. Correctly labeling your feelings.
5. Processing through your past experiences.
6. Identifying how you want to feel (i.e. resilience, emotional healing).
7. Identifying the skills you need to be resilient.
8. Practicing those skills so they can become a habit.

Journal Prompts for Self-awareness:

1. Why is it important to seek a therapist on your resilience journey?
2. What are the dangers in misdirected anger?
3. What are intentional decisions?
4. Who is responsible for your personal growth?
5. How can forgetting or suppression be harmful?
6. What are some examples of your brain's function?

CHAPTER 2

What blocks resilience?

It's important to figure out what blocks resilience because these barriers can keep you stuck in cycles of stress, self-doubt, and emotional overwhelm. Without understanding what's holding you back, whether it's fear of failure, negative self-talk, past trauma, or unhealthy coping mechanisms, you might continue reacting in ways that undermine your ability to bounce back from challenges. Identifying these blocks allows you to address them head-on, replace harmful patterns with healthier ones, and build the mental and emotional strength needed to navigate difficulties more effectively. In short, recognizing what hinders resilience is the first step toward strengthening it, leading to greater confidence, adaptability, and overall well-being.

Anxiety, depression, and trauma can block resilience by keeping the mind and body in a constant state of emotional distress, making it harder to cope with challenges in a healthy way. Below are insights about how each one can interfere with resilience:

1. **Anxiety** – Anxiety creates excessive worry and fear, often making obstacles seem bigger than they are. It keeps the brain in a hyper-alert state, making it difficult to think clearly, take risks, or trust in your ability to handle adversity. Instead of problem-solving, anxiety can lead to avoidance, which prevents growth and resilience-building.

2. **Depression** – Depression drains emotional and physical energy, making even small challenges feel overwhelming. It can lead to

hopelessness, negative self-talk, and a lack of motivation to push through difficulties. When someone feels emotionally numb or disconnected, it becomes harder to engage in the proactive behaviors needed to develop resilience.

3. **Trauma** – Trauma, whether from past experiences or ongoing stress, can keep the nervous system in survival mode, making it difficult to regulate emotions or trust in personal strength. It can lead to heightened emotional reactivity, difficulty forming supportive relationships, and an inability to see challenges as opportunities for growth. Instead of adapting and moving forward, trauma can make a person feel stuck in past pain.

Fear

Throughout my professional career, I have witnessed how fear can keep people trapped in a cycle of emotional and mental defeat. Many individuals remain stuck, not because they want to, but because fear convinces them that the unknown is more terrifying than their current reality—even if that reality is unhealthy. There is a strange sense of security in what is familiar, even when it causes pain or dysfunction. Over time, people learn to survive within their struggles simply because they don't know any other way.

For many, the idea of breaking free from deeply ingrained patterns or adopting a new mindset feels overwhelming, even impossible. The thought of change can bring up doubt, discomfort, and resistance because it challenges everything they've known. If they've never witnessed emotional regulation, self-compassion, or resilience in action, the idea of living differently might feel unrealistic. But growth begins with the willingness to question these fears and consider that a more fulfilling, balanced life *is* possible. The first step toward transformation is recognizing that fear doesn't have to be a barrier, it can be a signal that something greater is waiting on the other side of discomfort.

Recognizing fear can be helpful because it allows you to understand its purpose rather than be controlled by it. Fear is a natural response designed to protect you from danger, but in many cases, it holds you back from growth, change, and new opportunities. By identifying what you're afraid of, whether it's failure, rejection, or the unknown, you can begin to challenge those fears and determine whether they are based on real threats or simply limiting beliefs.

Once you recognize fear, you can shift from reacting impulsively to responding thoughtfully. Instead of letting it keep you stuck, you can use it as a tool for self-awareness. Fear can highlight areas where you need growth, show you what matters most, and even motivate you to build resilience. When faced head-on, fear loses its power and transforms into a stepping stone rather than a roadblock. Ultimately, recognizing fear gives you the ability to move forward with courage and confidence, rather than remaining trapped by uncertainty.

Self-trust is one of the most powerful tools for conquering fear because it shifts your focus from external uncertainties to your internal ability to handle challenges. When you trust yourself, you develop confidence in your decisions, emotions, and resilience, making fear feel less overwhelming. Instead of seeing fear as a stop sign, self-trust allows you to view it as a challenge you are capable of navigating. Self-trust helps you:

- Calm self-doubt – You believe in your ability to figure things out, even if the outcome is uncertain.
- Take risks with confidence – You no longer need absolute certainty before making a move because you trust yourself to adjust as needed.

- Recover from setbacks – You know that mistakes or failures are not the end, but learning experiences that you can grow from.

When you trust yourself more, you stop letting fear hold you back. You start believing in your own strength and ability to handle whatever comes your way. Fear doesn't completely go away, but it no longer controls your choices. Instead, you move forward with confidence, knowing that no matter what happens, you can handle it.

Building self-trust takes time, but with consistent effort, you'll develop the confidence to rely on yourself in any situation. Here are five ways to learn to trust yourself:

1. Keep small promises to yourself – Start by following through on simple commitments, like waking up at a set time or finishing a small task. Each time you keep a promise; you prove to yourself that you are reliable.

2. Listen to your intuition – Pay attention to your gut feelings instead of always seeking outside validation. Practice making small decisions without overthinking or asking for others' opinions.

3. Learn from mistakes instead of judging yourself – Instead of beating yourself up over failures, see them as lessons. Acknowledging that mistakes do not define your identity enhances confidence in your capacity to manage challenges and setbacks.

4. Set boundaries and honor them – Trusting yourself means respecting your own needs. When you set boundaries and stick to them, you show yourself that your feelings and well-being matter.

5. Speak kindly to yourself – Your inner voice plays a huge role in self-trust. Replace self-doubt with encouraging thoughts, and remind yourself that you are capable, strong, and worthy of trust.

Self-unaware

Being self-unaware can block resilience because it keeps you from recognizing the thoughts, emotions, and behaviors that may be holding you back. Without self-awareness, you might:

- Stay stuck in negative patterns – If you don't recognize unhealthy coping mechanisms, such as avoidance, self-doubt, or negative self-talk, you can't change them.
- React instead of responding – Without awareness of your emotions, you may be overly reactive, making decisions based on fear or frustration rather than thoughtful problem-solving.
- Struggle to learn from setbacks – Resilience grows when you reflect on challenges and adjust. If you're unaware of how you handle adversity, you may repeat mistakes instead of learning from them.
- Have difficulty setting boundaries – Self-awareness helps you understand your needs and limits. Without it, you might allow stress, toxic relationships, or burnout to take over.

Developing self-awareness is key to resilience because it helps you identify what's working, what's not, and what changes you need to make to grow stronger. When you understand yourself better, you gain the power to face challenges with clarity, confidence, and emotional balance.

Five ways to boost self-awareness:

1. Practice Mindfulness – Pay attention to your thoughts, emotions, and reactions in the present moment without judgment. This helps you recognize patterns and understand how you respond to different situations.

2. Journal Regularly – Writing down your thoughts, feelings, and experiences can help you identify recurring themes in your emotions and behavior, giving you deeper insight into yourself.

3. Ask for Honest Feedback – Sometimes, others can see things we miss about ourselves. Ask trusted friends, family, or mentors for constructive feedback about your strengths and areas for growth.

4. Reflect on Your Reactions – When you feel a strong emotional response to something, take a moment to ask yourself why. What triggered it? Is it based on past experiences? Understanding your reactions helps you gain better emotional control.

5. Identify Your Values and Beliefs – Take time to clarify what truly matters to you. When you know your core values, you can align your actions with them, making more intentional and fulfilling choices.

Not Understanding Your Authentic Self

Understanding your authentic self is crucial for resilience because it gives you a solid foundation to navigate challenges with confidence and clarity. When you know who you truly are, your values, strengths, weaknesses, and triggers, you're better equipped to face adversity in a way that aligns with your core beliefs and strengths.

Clarity in Decision-Making

When you understand your authentic self, making decisions becomes much clearer. You have a solid sense of what you value, what matters to you, and what aligns with your long-term goals. This clarity allows you to make choices that are true to your core beliefs, even when faced with difficult circumstances. Instead of being swayed by external pressures or fear of judgment, you can confidently move forward knowing that your decisions reflect who you really are. This strong sense of direction keeps you grounded, reducing feelings of doubt and helping you stay focused on what's truly important, even in times of uncertainty.

Emotional Awareness

Understanding your authentic self leads to a deeper emotional awareness. You become more attuned to how you're feeling in various situations, and more importantly, why you feel that way. This awareness allows you to catch emotions early, before they spiral out of control, and gives you the tools to manage them more effectively. Instead of being overwhelmed or reactive, you can pause, assess the situation, and respond thoughtfully. Being in touch with your emotions also helps you avoid negative patterns of behavior, like overreacting or shutting down, which can block your ability to bounce back from challenges.

Self-Compassion

Knowing and accepting your authentic self-promotes self-compassion, which is essential for resilience. When you embrace who you truly are, including your imperfections, you develop a kinder, more forgiving attitude toward yourself. This is particularly important during tough times when you might feel like you've failed or aren't measuring up. Instead of beating yourself up, you can recognize that setbacks are a normal part of growth and not a reflection of your worth. Self-compassion allows you to be patient with yourself, bounce back more quickly, and keep trying, knowing that your worth isn't defined by your mistakes or struggles.

Increased Confidence

Self-awareness naturally leads to increased confidence because you're no longer trying to meet external expectations or live up to someone else's idea of success. When you truly understand your strengths and limitations, you can trust in your abilities and make choices based on what feels right for you, not based on seeking approval. This self-assurance gives you the resilience to face challenges head-on, knowing that you can handle whatever comes your way. Confidence in your authentic self also allows you to take risks, face adversity with a positive mindset, and keep pushing forward, even when things get tough.

Staying Grounded in Adversity

When you understand your authentic self, you develop an inner stability that helps you stay grounded, no matter what life throws at you. Adversity often causes people to question their worth, second-guess their decisions, or lose sight of what's important. But when you're aligned with who you truly are, you can stay centered even in the most chaotic moments. Your sense of self becomes a source of strength, helping you navigate difficult times with a clear sense of purpose. Knowing your authentic self means that, no matter how challenging life gets, you always have a solid foundation to return to, allowing you to bounce back faster and more effectively.

By practicing these steps consistently, you'll develop a deeper understanding of yourself:

1. **Practice Mindfulness**

   Mindfulness helps you become more aware of your thoughts, emotions, and reactions in the present moment. Set aside time each day to observe how you're feeling without judgment. Whether through meditation, deep breathing, or simply pausing to check in with yourself, mindfulness allows you to recognize patterns in your emotions and behaviors, helping you understand yourself on a deeper level.

2. Keep a Reflection Journal

Writing down your thoughts and experiences can provide valuable insights into your emotions, triggers, and decision-making processes. Each day, take a few minutes to reflect on what you felt, what challenges you faced, and how you reacted. Over time, patterns will emerge, showing you where you thrive and where you might need growth. Journaling also helps you track progress in your personal development journey.

3. Seek Honest Feedback

Sometimes, we have blind spots when it comes to understanding ourselves. Asking trusted friends, family members, or mentors for honest feedback can provide an outside perspective on your strengths and areas for improvement. Be open to constructive criticism and use it as a tool for growth rather than taking it personally. Gaining insight from others can help you see yourself more clearly.

4. Identify Your Core Values

Understanding what truly matters to you is key to self-awareness. Take time to reflect on your core values, the beliefs and principles that guide your decisions and actions. Are you living in alignment with them? If not, where can you make adjustments? When you know your values, you gain a stronger sense of direction and purpose, making it easier to stay true to yourself in all areas of life.

5. Analyze Your Reactions and Triggers

Pay attention to situations that cause strong emotional reactions, whether positive or negative. Ask yourself why a certain event, comment, or challenge triggered such a response. Is it linked to past experiences? Is it revealing an insecurity or a deeply held belief? Understanding your triggers allows you to manage emotions more effectively, reducing impulsive reactions and increasing emotional resilience.

Rejection

Rejection and lack of resilience are closely connected because rejection can be emotionally painful, and without resilience, it can feel overwhelming, discouraging, or even defining. Building resilience helps you handle rejection without losing confidence, keeping you motivated and open to new experiences rather than allowing setbacks to define your self-worth. Rejection can damage self-worth. Without resilience, rejection can feel like proof that you're not good enough, leading to self-doubt and a fear of trying again. A resilient mindset, however, helps you see rejection as a part of life rather than a reflection of your value.

Fear of rejection can lead to avoidance. If you struggle with resilience, you may avoid taking healthy risks, whether in relationships, careers, or personal growth out of fear of being rejected. This avoidance can limit opportunities and keep you stuck in your comfort zone. Rejection can trigger negative self-talk. Without resilience, rejection can fuel harsh inner criticism, reinforcing beliefs like *"I'm not worthy"* or *"I'll never succeed."* Resilience helps you challenge these thoughts and replace them with a healthier perspective. Lack of resilience prolongs emotional recovery. Everyone experiences rejection, but those with low resilience tend to dwell on it longer, making it harder to move forward. Resilience helps you process rejection, learn from it, and shift focus on new opportunities.

Resilience turns rejection into growth. When you build resilience, you see rejection as feedback, not failure. Instead of letting it break you down, you use it as a lesson to improve, adapt, and try again with greater strength and confidence.

1. Acknowledge Your Feelings

Rejection hurts, and it's okay to feel disappointed, sad, or frustrated. Instead of suppressing your emotions, allow yourself to process them. Write about how you feel, talk to someone you trust, or simply sit with your emotions without judgment. Acknowledging your feelings is the first step to moving past them.

2. Challenge Negative Self-Talk

Rejection can trigger harsh self-criticism, like "I'm not good enough" or "I'll never succeed." Instead of letting these thoughts take over, challenge them. Ask yourself: Is this thought based on facts or just emotions? Reframe rejection as a learning experience rather than a reflection of your worth.

3. Gain Perspective

Rejection often feels personal, but it's not always about you. Maybe you weren't the right fit for a job, a relationship, or an opportunity at that moment. Remind yourself that rejection is a natural part of life and doesn't define your abilities or potential. Sometimes, it's simply a redirection toward something better suited for you.

4. Focus on Self-Improvement

Instead of dwelling on the rejection, use it as motivation to grow. Reflect on what you can learn from the experience and what adjustments you might make moving forward. Whether it's developing a skill, improving communication, or shifting your approach, turning rejection into a learning opportunity helps you come back stronger.

5. Keep Moving Forward

The best way to overcome rejection is to not let it stop you. Keep applying for new jobs, meeting new people, or pursuing your goals despite setbacks. Every successful person has faced rejection, but resilience is what keeps them going. Trust that each rejection brings you one step closer to the right opportunity.

CHAPTER 3

Intrusive thoughts, feelings, and self-forgiveness

Throughout my professional experience, intrusive thoughts have been a frequent topic of conversation. These unwanted, often distressing thoughts can become overwhelming, growing in intensity over time. When left unchecked, their persistence can lead to emotional exhaustion, increased anxiety, and even self-doubt. What makes intrusive thoughts particularly burdensome is that they often feel natural, which can make them seem true, even when they are not.

One of the biggest struggles people face with intrusive thoughts is the fear that these thoughts reflect their true beliefs or character. Since they arise automatically and repeatedly, they can create a false sense of reality. The more a thought is repeated, the more familiar it becomes, and the brain tends to associate familiarity with truth. This is why negative, self-critical, or fear-based thoughts can feel so powerful. Over time, they can shape how a person perceives themselves and the world, reinforcing unhealthy thought patterns.

Just like any habit, intrusive thoughts gain strength through repetition. A habit forms when an action or thought is repeated enough times that it becomes ingrained in the mind. The same principle applies to intrusive thinking—if certain negative thoughts continue to surface without being challenged, they can start to feel automatic and inescapable. However, just as unhealthy thought patterns can develop through repetition, they can also be *rewired* through intentional practice. Recognizing that intrusive thoughts are not truths, but rather mental habits, is the first step toward breaking free from their hold.

Recognizing that intrusive thoughts are mental habits helps you regain control over them because, like any habit, they can be changed. Just as negative thought patterns develop through repetition, new, healthier habits can be built in their place. This shift in perspective empowers you to see intrusive thoughts not as an unchangeable part of who you are, but as a mental pattern that can be rewired with conscious effort.

By actively working to replace intrusive thoughts with more constructive ones, you can train your brain to respond differently. This process might involve techniques such as mindfulness, cognitive reframing, or self-compassion exercises. For example, instead of automatically accepting a negative thought as truth, you can pause, question its validity, and consciously choose a more balanced or positive perspective. Over time, the brain adapts, and the new way of thinking starts to feel more natural, just like any habit that is practiced consistently.

Additionally, changing mental habits goes beyond just altering thoughts—it also involves creating new behaviors that reinforce positive thinking. Engaging in activities that promote emotional well-being, such as journaling, meditation, exercise, or speaking kindly to yourself, helps strengthen the new mental pathways you are building. The more you practice these habits, the more they become second nature, gradually replacing intrusive thoughts with healthier and more empowering ones. Thought patterns are not set in stone. With patience and persistence, you can reshape your mental habits, giving yourself the power to break free from intrusive thoughts and regain control over your mind.

One of the most powerful ways to change your thought patterns and regain control over your mind is to stop being afraid of your thoughts.

Fear gives intrusive thoughts more power, making them feel even more overwhelming and inescapable. Instead of pushing them away or avoiding them, try to face them with curiosity rather than fear. When you acknowledge and examine your thoughts without judgment, you begin to understand that they are just mental events, not absolute truths.

A crucial part of this process is listening to your internal dialogue. Pay close attention to the way you speak to yourself when intrusive thoughts arise. Are you harsh and self-critical, telling yourself things like "I don't deserve this promotion," "Something must be wrong with me," or "I can't control my mind"? Or do you approach yourself with kindness, saying "This is just a thought, and I don't have to believe it," "I am in control of how I respond," or "I can choose a different perspective"? The way you talk to yourself shapes the way you experience your thoughts, so shifting your inner dialogue from fear-based to compassionate can make a huge difference.

Instead of fighting intrusive thoughts, try to observe them as if you were watching clouds pass in the sky. Remind yourself that thoughts are not commands, they are just mental noise that comes and goes. The more you detach from them and respond with self-awareness and self-compassion; the less control they will have over you. With practice, you'll start replacing negative mental habits with ones that empower and support you, ultimately giving you the confidence to reclaim control over your thoughts and emotions.

Overcoming intrusive thoughts and replacing them with healthier, more positive ones requires self-love, self-care, patience, and a gentle approach toward yourself. It's easy to become frustrated or even angry when intrusive thoughts appear, but reacting with agitation or self-criticism only reinforces their power. Instead of trying to force them away or punishing yourself for having them, meet them with kindness and understanding. Self-love means reminding yourself that intrusive thoughts do not define you. They are simply mental patterns, habits that have formed over time, and like any habit, they can be changed. Treat yourself with the same compassion you would offer a friend who is struggling. Self-care plays a crucial role in this process as well. Engaging in activities that nourish your mind and body, such as exercise, meditation, journaling, or deep breathing, helps you create a healthier mental space where intrusive thoughts have less control.

Patience is key because changing thought patterns don't happen overnight. Just as intrusive thoughts become strong through repetition, replacing them with healthier ones requires consistent effort and time. Some days will feel easier than others, and that's okay. Progress is not about perfection, it's about making small, intentional choices every day that move you toward a more balanced and peaceful state of mind. Most importantly, avoid frustration with yourself. It's easy to fall into the trap of thinking, "Why am I still struggling with this?" or "I should be over this by now." But healing is not linear. Instead of reacting with agitation, remind yourself that every step forward—no matter how small—is still progress. The more you approach yourself with compassion rather than criticism, the easier it becomes to break free from intrusive thoughts and replace them with thoughts that support and uplift you.

Understanding your Feelings

Understanding your feelings is crucial for resilience because emotions provide valuable insight into how you respond to challenges and stress. When you are aware of your emotions, you can manage them effectively rather than letting them control you. Resilience isn't about avoiding difficult emotions, it's about recognizing, processing, and navigating them in a healthy way. By tuning into your feelings instead of ignoring or fearing them, you build emotional intelligence, which is a key foundation for resilience. The better you understand yourself emotionally, the more effectively you can handle life's challenges with confidence and balance.

Why emotional awareness strengthens resilience:

1. **Prevents Emotional Overload** – When you understand your feelings, you can address them before they become overwhelming. Suppressing emotions can lead to anxiety, stress, or burnout, making it harder to bounce back from setbacks.

2. **Improves Problem-Solving** – Resilient people don't let emotions cloud their judgment; they use emotions as signals to help them make thoughtful decisions. Recognizing frustration, sadness, or fear allows you to respond logically rather than react impulsively.

3. **Enhances Emotional Regulation** – Self-awareness helps you manage emotions rather than being controlled by them. Instead of feeling stuck in sadness, anger, or self-doubt, you learn to process these emotions and shift toward a more constructive mindset.

4. **Strengthens Relationships** – Understanding your emotions makes it easier to communicate your needs, set boundaries, and form healthy connections. Supportive relationships are a key part of resilience, and emotional awareness helps you maintain them.

5. **Encourages Growth and Adaptability** – When you face difficulties, your emotions can guide you toward solutions. Instead of seeing setbacks as failures, emotional awareness allows

you to view them as learning experiences, helping you grow stronger and more adaptable over time.

Feelings are natural responses to life experiences, shaping how we interpret and react to the world around us. In the present moment, emotions arise as a reflection of what we are experiencing, joy from a kind gesture, frustration from a setback, or sadness from a loss. However, when we continue to feel the same emotions long after the initial experience has passed, it can feel as though we are re-living the event repeatedly. Instead of moving forward, we remain stuck in a cycle of self-punishment, reinforcing negative thoughts and fears that keep us from healing. When we dwell in past pain, our minds begin to internalize those emotions as part of our identity. We may start to believe we don't deserve happiness, love, or success. This can create unhealthy attachments to negative emotions, making fear, shame, or self-doubt feel familiar, even comfortable. Over time, this can shape how we see ourselves and the world, keeping us trapped in patterns of avoidance, self-sabotage, or low self-worth.

The key to breaking free from this cycle is learning to accept emotions without judgment. Instead of criticizing yourself for feeling sad, anxious, or afraid, practice giving yourself grace and forgiveness. Feelings are not weaknesses, and they do not define your worth. They are simply signals, guiding you toward areas that need attention, healing, or change. By acknowledging them with kindness rather than fear, you allow yourself to process emotions in a healthy way rather than being controlled by them. Healing, growth, and resilience come from facing emotions, not avoiding them. By embracing your feelings with self-compassion and understanding, you regain power over your own story, transforming pain into strength and challenges into opportunities for growth.

What is Self-forgiveness?

Self-forgiveness is essential for true resilience because it allows you to move forward without being weighed down by guilt, shame, or self-judgment. Holding onto past mistakes or regrets can keep you emotionally stuck, preventing you from growing, adapting, and facing new challenges with confidence. Resilience isn't just about bouncing back, it's about learning, evolving, and continuing forward despite setbacks. By practicing self-forgiveness, you cultivate emotional resilience, self-trust, and the courage to face challenges without fear of imperfection. Instead of dwelling on what went wrong, you give yourself the grace to keep moving forward, stronger and wiser than before.

Self-forgiveness strengthens resilience:

1. **Breaks the Cycle of Self-Punishment**

    Without self-forgiveness, mistakes don't just remain in the past, they become part of an ongoing internal dialogue that reinforces self-doubt and unworthiness. The more you replay your perceived failures, the more they shape your self-image, leading to a cycle of guilt, shame, and negative self-talk. This emotional burden makes it difficult to take risks, try new things, or believe in your ability to succeed. Self-forgiveness interrupts this cycle by reminding you that everyone makes mistakes, and that missteps are not a reflection of your worth. Letting go of self-punishment helps you focus on growth rather than guilt, allowing you to move forward with a healthier mindset.

2. **Encourages Growth and Learning**

    Resilience is about adapting and improving after setbacks, but that's nearly impossible if you are stuck in self-condemnation. When you forgive yourself, you shift from a fixed mindset (believing failure defines you) to a growth mindset (believing failure teaches you). Instead of dwelling on what went wrong, you ask, "What can I learn from this?" This perspective turns mistakes into stepping stones for personal development, helping you build the emotional flexibility needed to navigate future challenges. Self-forgiveness also encourages self-reflection, allowing you to recognize patterns, adjust behaviors, and make wiser decisions moving forward.

3. Reduces Emotional Baggage

Unforgiveness is emotional weight that keeps you tethered to the past. The more guilt and regret you carry, the less energy you must focus on the present or prepare for the future. Emotional baggage can manifest stress, anxiety, and even physical symptoms like fatigue or tension. Over time, unresolved guilt can make even small obstacles feel overwhelming because your mind is already burdened by past mistakes. Self-forgiveness acts as an emotional reset, allowing you to release unnecessary burdens and regain mental clarity. When you free yourself from the weight of regret, you create space for renewed energy, motivation, and resilience in the face of new challenges.

4. Promotes Self-Compassion and Emotional Strength

True resilience isn't about perfection or never making mistakes, it's about how you treat yourself when things don't go as planned. Self-compassion is the key to emotional strength because it allows you to face difficulties without fear of self-judgment. When you forgive yourself, you build emotional security, knowing that you can handle setbacks without tearing yourself down. This self-kindness fosters a sense of inner stability, which helps you remain calm and centered even in difficult situations. The more you practice self-forgiveness, the more confident you become in your ability to navigate life's ups and downs with resilience and grace.

5. Empowers You to Keep Moving Forward

Resilience is all about persistence, continuing despite setbacks. If you are stuck in self-blame and regret, it's easy to become paralyzed by fear, avoiding risks because you don't trust yourself to handle failure. Self-forgiveness frees you from this paralysis by reminding you that mistakes do not define you, your response to them does. When you forgive yourself, you rebuild self-trust and recognize that no setback is permanent. This sense of self-empowerment allows you to keep pushing forward, taking risks, and embracing new opportunities without fear of imperfection.

Self-forgiveness cannot truly begin until you break free from the cycle of self-punishment. This cycle follows a predictable pattern:

(A) The Thought – "I made a mistake, so I must be a bad person."

It starts with negative thought, guilt, shame, or self-doubt creeping in, convincing you that you are unworthy or incapable of change. This thought becomes intrusive, repeating itself until it feels like truth.

(B) The Behavior – "Since I already feel this way, I might as well act accordingly."

Because the thought feels so real, it often leads to behaviors that reinforce it. This could be self-sabotage, avoidance, withdrawing from others, or even engaging in destructive habits. You may convince yourself that change is impossible, so you give in to old patterns.

(C) The Consequence (Self-Punishment) – "Now I've proven I was right about myself."

This behavior leads to a consequence, further reinforcing feelings of guilt, shame, or failure. The negative thought at the beginning of the cycle now seems even more valid because your actions aligned with it. This creates a self-fulfilling prophecy, keeping you trapped in self-punishment and making self-forgiveness feel out of reach.

Breaking the Cycle

To truly begin self-forgiveness, you must first interrupt this cycle. It starts with challenging (A) the thought before it dictates (B) your behavior and leads to (C) self-punishment. Instead of believing, "I can't change, so I deserve this pain," you shift your mindset to, "I made a mistake, but I am capable of growth." You don't have to "deserve" self-forgiveness, it's something you allow yourself. The moment you stop punishing yourself and start seeing mistakes as opportunities to learn, you take back control. Self-forgiveness is not about ignoring the past, it's about freeing yourself from the weight of it so you can move forward with strength, resilience, and self-compassion.

Another important factor in breaking the cycle of self-punishment and embracing self- forgiveness is recognizing your dominant inner voice, who are you truly listening to? We all have an internal dialogue, but often, that voice is shaped by past experiences, societal expectations, or the words of others rather than our true selves. If your dominant voice is self-critical, filled with doubt, or echoing past judgments, it will keep reinforcing negative thoughts and preventing you from healing.

Whose Voice Is Leading You?

- Is it the voice of self-judgment, telling you that you're not good enough?
- Is it the voice of perfectionism, making you feel like mistakes are failures rather than learning experiences?
- Is it the voice of fear, convincing you that change is impossible?
- Or is it the voice of self-compassion, reminding you that growth takes up time and that you are worthy of grace?

Shifting to a Healthier Inner Voice

If you constantly listen to the voice of self-criticism, you will remain stuck in self-punishment. However, when you actively work to shift your dominant voice to one of kindness, encouragement, and resilience, you create the space needed for true self-forgiveness.

This shift requires intention and practice:

- Challenge negative thoughts the moment they appear.
- Replace harsh self-talk with supportive and constructive language.
- Speak to yourself the way you would a close friend in pain.
- Surround yourself with people who reinforce healthy, positive perspectives.

By changing the voice you listen to most, you take control of your narrative and start leading with self-trust and self-compassion, both essential for resilience and emotional healing.

CHAPTER 4

Resilience and Anxiety

From a neuroscience perspective, anxiety is a complex emotional and physiological response that involves the brain's processing of perceived threats and the activation of stress pathways. The primary regions of the brain involved in anxiety include the amygdala, prefrontal cortex, and hippocampus.

1. **Amygdala**

   The amygdala plays a central role in detecting threats and triggering the body's fight-or-flight response. When we encounter a stressful or fear-inducing stimulus, the amygdala rapidly processes it and sends signals to other parts of the brain and body to prepare for action. In individuals with anxiety, the amygdala may be hyperactive, leading to exaggerated or prolonged stress responses even in situations where there is no real danger.

2. **Prefrontal Cortex**

   The prefrontal cortex (PFC) is involved in higher-order cognitive functions, including decision-making, regulation of emotions, and assessing risk. In a healthy stress response, the prefrontal cortex helps regulate the amygdala's reaction by assessing whether the threat is real and how to respond appropriately. However, in individuals with anxiety, the PFC may not sufficiently regulate the amygdala, leading to overactive emotional responses.

3. Hippocampus

The hippocampus is crucial for memory and learning, especially in processing past experiences. In anxiety, the hippocampus may contribute to the brain's tendency to over-interpret past traumatic or stressful experiences, which can lead to anticipatory anxiety (fear of future events based on past experiences). A reduced hippocampal volume has been observed in individuals with chronic anxiety, which may contribute to difficulties in distinguishing real threats from perceived ones.

4. Neurotransmitters

Anxiety is also linked to imbalances in certain neurotransmitters, particularly serotonin, gamma-aminobutyric acid (GABA), and norepinephrine. Serotonin plays a role in mood regulation, and a deficiency in serotonin is often seen in anxiety and mood disorders. GABA, an inhibitory neurotransmitter, helps calm the brain's overactive signals, and lower GABA activity is associated with heightened anxiety. Norepinephrine, which is involved in the body's stress response, can be dysregulated in anxiety, leading to an increased physical and emotional reaction to stress.

(Bishop, S. J. (2007). Neurocognitive mechanisms of anxiety: An integrative account of the emotional brain. Murray, E. A., & Izquierdo, A. (2007). The role of the prefrontal cortex in working memory and decision-making.)

I wanted to include the neuroscience behind anxiety in my book because it's important to understand that anxiety isn't just something that appears out of nowhere, it's deeply connected to how we process and interpret the world around us. It's not just an emotional state but a biological response that affects the way we view ourselves and the world. Anxiety shapes how we make decisions, often causing us to overanalyze or hesitate, fearing the worst possible outcomes. It also influences how we experience and manage emotions, with the brain's response to fear or stress impacting everything from our reactions to everyday challenges to how we process past experiences. By understanding the neuroscience of anxiety, we can see that it's not just an internal struggle but a complex interaction between brain function, emotional regulation, and thought patterns, making it an issue that deserves both understanding and care.

So, how do you know if you have anxiety? According to the DSM-5 (Diagnostic and Statistical Manual of Mental Disorders, 5th Edition), anxiety disorders are characterized by excessive worry, fear, or nervousness that interfere with daily functioning. If your anxiety causes significant distress or impairment in your life, whether it's affecting your relationships, work, or daily activities, it's important to seek help from a healthcare provider. You may be experiencing anxiety if your symptoms align with the DSM-5 criteria, but only a mental health professional can provide a full assessment and formal diagnosis.

General Criteria for Anxiety Disorders:

1. **Excessive and Persistent Worry or Fear:**

   - You experience chronic worry or fear that is disproportionate to the situation at hand.
   - These feelings occur more days than not for at least 6 months and are difficult to control.

2. **Physical Symptoms:**

Anxiety is not just a mental experience—it also manifests physically. Symptoms might include:

- **Restlessness**
- **Fatigue**
- **Muscle tension**
- **Difficulty concentrating**
- **Sleep disturbances** (trouble falling asleep or staying asleep)
- **Irritability**

3. Avoidance:

- You may avoid certain situations, places, or activities because they trigger anxiety, which can impact your day-to-day life.

4. Impairment in Functioning:

- Anxiety or related behaviors interfere with your work, social life, or other important areas of functioning. For example, it might make it difficult to carry out daily tasks or engage in social activities.

Anxiety is a natural response that is hardwired into the brain for survival. It's part of the body's fight-or-flight mechanism, which evolved to keep us safe from real threats. When faced with danger, the brain signals the body to either fight, flee, or freeze. This automatic reaction helps us respond quickly to perceived threats. In moderation, anxiety can be helpful, alerting us to danger, motivating us to prepare for important events, or encouraging us to act. The goal is not to eliminate anxiety entirely but to manage it in a way that prevents it from interfering with daily life and well-being. Just as we learn to manage physical health conditions, we can also develop tools to manage anxiety, creating a more balanced, resilient approach to life.

However, just like headaches or a cold, anxiety isn't something that is "cured," but instead, it needs to be managed. Chronic or excessive anxiety, like recurring headaches or frequent colds, becomes disruptive, often out of proportion to the actual threat. In these cases, anxiety management strategies—such as therapy, medication, mindfulness, or lifestyle adjustments—become essential for maintaining a healthy balance.

For some, medications like antidepressants or anti-anxiety medications can help manage the brain's overactive response. These medications don't "cure" anxiety but can regulate neurotransmitter activity, making it easier to manage the symptoms and feel more in control. Similarly, therapeutic approaches such as cognitive-behavioral therapy (CBT) can help individuals reframe anxious thoughts and reduce their intensity over time.

Positive and Negative Reinforcement

Positive reinforcement and negative reinforcement are psychological concepts rooted in operant conditioning, a theory that explains how behaviors are influenced by rewards or consequences. These principles can be helpful in understanding how anxiety is reinforced, and how building resilience involves using these strategies in healthier, more constructive ways.

Positive reinforcement occurs when a behavior is followed by a pleasant stimulus or reward, which increases the likelihood of that behavior being repeated. In the context of anxiety, positive reinforcement can sometimes inadvertently reinforce avoidance behaviors. For example, if someone experiences anxiety in a social situation and avoids it, the relief they feel by avoiding the anxiety-inducing situation can reinforce avoidance behavior, making it more likely that they will avoid similar situations in the future. In this case, the reward is temporary relief from anxiety. While this may feel good in the moment, over time, the reinforcement of avoidance leads to increased anxiety in future situations and further limits the person's opportunities for growth.

Building resilience requires recognizing when positive reinforcement is inadvertently reinforcing anxious or unhelpful behaviors. Instead of avoiding situations, facing fears gradually can help reframe how the brain responds. By rewarding yourself for facing anxiety-provoking situations, even in small steps, you gradually build confidence and resilience. Positive reinforcement can also be used constructively to encourage healthy coping mechanisms like relaxation techniques, problem-solving, and seeking support, reinforcing these adaptive behaviors rather than avoidance.

Negative reinforcement involves the removal of an unpleasant stimulus after a behavior, which also increases the likelihood of that behavior being repeated. In the case of anxiety, negative reinforcement often involves avoiding discomfort or anxiety-provoking situations, which relieves stress or fear temporarily but reinforces the anxious response over time. For instance, if someone feels anxious about public speaking and practices avoidance (such as not speaking in front of others), the immediate relief from anxiety can serve as a negative reinforcement, which strengthens avoidance behaviors. Over time, this can make the person feel even less capable of handling anxiety-provoking situations.

Building resilience involves breaking the cycle of negative reinforcement. Instead of seeking immediate relief through avoidance or safety behaviors, it's important to face the anxiety and tolerate the discomfort, knowing that it will decrease over time. By allowing yourself to experience discomfort in small, manageable doses and rewarding progress (even if it's incremental), you shift the focus from short-term relief to long-term growth. This process helps you build tolerance to anxiety and reinforces healthier coping mechanisms, which strengthens your ability to bounce back from challenges.

If you notice yourself avoiding anxiety-provoking situations, acknowledge that avoidance may be reinforcing the anxiety, rather than alleviating it in the long run. Practice gradual exposure to these situations, reinforcing the ability to tolerate discomfort. Use positive reinforcement to encourage healthy coping behaviors, such as breathing exercises, seeking social support, or reframing negative thoughts. Celebrate small victories along the way to build confidence in your ability to handle anxiety. Instead of seeing anxiety as something to avoid at all costs, begin to view it as a natural response that can be managed. Use your experiences of anxiety to build your emotional muscle, rather than seeking to eliminate it. In doing so, you teach your brain that it can handle anxiety and come out stronger.

Anxiety and depression symptoms can fluctuate over time, some days may feel easier, while others feel overwhelming. However, these emotions often circle back because they are a natural part of human experience, just like physical discomforts such as headaches or the common cold. There is no permanent cure for emotions, just as there is no cure for a headache. Instead, we learn to manage and reduce their intensity through healthy habits and self-care.

Think of it this way: when we get a cold, we might take precautions such as eating well, getting enough sleep, avoiding germs, but sometimes, despite our best efforts, we still catch a cold. However, we don't blame the current cold on the last time we were sick—we recognize that illness comes and goes. Yet, with anxiety and sadness, we often mentally link today's feelings to past struggles, creating a cycle of distress where we expect the emotions to spiral or linger longer than they need to.

By isolating the reaction, meaning recognizing anxiety or sadness as a temporary experience rather than part of a never-ending pattern, we can lessen its intensity. Instead of saying, "Here it comes again, just like last time," try shifting your mindset to, "This is just a moment. It will pass." This shift in thinking gives you more control over your emotional response, helping you regulate emotions without feeling trapped in a cycle of fear or distress. Just like we manage physical health by staying hydrated, eating well, and resting, we can manage emotional well-being by practicing self-awareness, mindfulness, and self-regulation techniques. The goal is not to eliminate difficult emotions but to reduce their impact and build resilience, so they no longer feel overpowered.

Procrastination

Procrastination is closely linked to both anxiety and resilience because it often serves as a coping mechanism for avoiding discomfort, uncertainty, or fear of failure. While it may provide temporary relief, procrastination ultimately reinforces negative thought patterns, increases stress, and weakens resilience over time.

How procrastination relates to anxiety:

1. Avoidance as a coping mechanism: Procrastination is often a response to fear and anxiety, fear of failure, fear of imperfection, or fear of the unknown. When a task feels overwhelming, avoiding it provides short-term relief. However, this avoidance reinforces the idea that the task is too difficult to face, increasing anxiety when it inevitably has to be completed.

2. Increases stress and guilt: While procrastination may ease anxiety in the moment, it creates long-term stress. The looming deadline or unfinished responsibility remains in the back of the mind, building pressure. This cycle can lead to feelings of guilt and self-doubt, which further fuel anxiety and make it even harder to take action.

3. <u>Perfectionism and overthinking</u>: Many people with anxiety struggle with perfectionism, which can make starting a task feel overwhelming. They may fear that if they don't do something perfectly, they will fail, leading them to delay starting at all. This overthinking can paralyze decision-making and make even simple tasks feel impossible.

How procrastination affects resilience:

1. <u>Weakens self-trust:</u> Resilience relies on self-trust, the belief that you can handle challenges and adapt to difficulties. Procrastination weakens this self-trust by reinforcing the idea that you cannot face discomfort head-on. Over time, this can create a sense of helplessness, making it harder to bounce back from setbacks.

2. <u>Reinforces negative thought patterns:</u> Every time procrastination leads to stress or failure, it reinforces self-doubt and avoidance behaviors. Instead of developing the ability to push through difficulties, the brain learns that avoiding challenges is an easier (but damaging) solution. This can make it harder to develop the resilience needed to handle stress effectively.

3. <u>Reduces emotional tolerance</u>: Resilient people face discomfort and push through it, while chronic procrastination lowers emotional tolerance for stress, discomfort, and uncertainty. Over time, avoiding hard tasks can make them seem even more intimidating, reducing confidence in one's ability to manage future challenges.

Procrastination and anxiety reinforce each other in a cycle that can weaken resilience. However, by recognizing procrastination as an avoidance behavior rather than a personal flaw, you can begin to break the pattern. Developing resilience means facing discomfort, challenging negative thoughts, and building trust in your ability to handle difficult situations. The more you push through anxiety-driven procrastination, the stronger and more resilient you become.

Building Resilience by Overcoming Procrastination:

- Practice Self-Compassion – Instead of criticizing yourself for procrastinating, recognize that it's a coping mechanism for anxiety. Approach yourself with kindness and focus on progress, not perfection.
- Use the "5-Minute Rule" – Tell yourself you'll work on a task for just five minutes. Often, getting started is the hardest part, and once momentum builds, anxiety decreases.
- Reframe Failure – View mistakes as learning opportunities rather than proof of inadequacy. This shift in mindset reduces fear-based procrastination and strengthens resilience.
- Break Tasks into Small Steps – Overwhelming tasks contribute to avoidance. Breaking them into small, manageable pieces makes them feel more doable, reducing anxiety and reinforcing resilience.
- Recognize the Long-Term Impact – Instead of focusing on the short-term relief of avoidance, remind yourself that taking action now builds long-term confidence and self-trust.

Whole-body Approach

To effectively manage anxiety and build resilience, we must learn how to calm the nervous system using a whole-body approach, one that considers not just our physical responses, but also our mental and emotional well-being. Anxiety is not just "in our head", it affects the entire body, from our heart rate and breathing patterns to our muscle tension and digestion. That's why a holistic approach is necessary, focusing on both regulating the body's stress response and monitoring and changing thought patterns that contribute to anxiety.

1. Regulating the nervous system physically

Since anxiety triggers the fight-or-flight response, calming the nervous system requires activating the parasympathetic nervous system (the body's relaxation mode). This can be done through:

- Deep breathing techniques – slow, controlled breathing sends signals to the brain that there is no immediate threat, helping to slow the heart rate and relax the body.
- Movement and exercise – physical activity, such as yoga, stretching, walking, or strength training, releases tension and lowers cortisol levels (the stress hormone), making it easier for the body to shift out of an anxious state.
- Proper sleep and nutrition – Lack of sleep and poor nutrition can increase inflammation and stress hormones, making the nervous system more reactive to anxiety. Prioritizing restorative sleep, balanced meals, and hydration helps stabilize mood and energy levels.

2. Monitoring thoughts: recognizing anxiety-driven thinking

Anxiety is often fueled by negative thought patterns, such as catastrophizing (*"Everything will go wrong"*), black-and-white thinking (*"If I fail at this, I'm a failure"*), or overgeneralizing (*"Bad things always happen to me"*). Learning to monitor your thoughts involves becoming more aware of these distortions and catching them before they spiral into fear-based decision-making.

- Journaling can help track thought patterns and identify recurring negative beliefs.

- Mindfulness practices allow you to observe your thoughts without judgment, rather than getting caught up in them.

3. Changing thought patterns: rewiring the brain

Once we recognize unhelpful thought patterns, the next step is changing them. This involves:

- Cognitive Reframing – Instead of accepting anxious thoughts as truth, challenge them: "Is there real evidence for this fear, or is my anxiety exaggerating the risk?"
- Positive Self-Talk – Replace self-criticism with compassionate, empowering language. Instead of "I can't handle this," shift to "I am capable of getting through this, one step at a time."
- Exposure to Discomfort – Gradually facing anxiety-inducing situations in small, manageable steps helps retrain the brain to see them as less threatening, strengthening emotional resilience over time.

CHAPTER 5

Resilience and Depression

According to the DSM-5 (Diagnostic and Statistical Manual of Mental Disorders, 5th Edition), Major Depressive Disorder (MDD) is diagnosed when a person experiences at least five or more symptoms for a minimum of two weeks, and these symptoms cause significant distress or impairment in daily life (work, relationships, or personal functioning), and depressive episode cannot be attributed to substance use, medical conditions, or another mental disorder (such as bipolar disorder). Remember, only a health professional can provide a diagnosis.

To be diagnosed with clinical depression, you must experience five or more of the following symptoms nearly every day for at least two weeks, with at least one of the symptoms being (1) depressed mood or (2) loss of interest or pleasure:

- Depressed Mood – Feeling sad, empty, hopeless, or down for most of the day. In children or adolescents, this may manifest as irritability rather than sadness.
- Loss of Interest or Pleasure (Anhedonia) – A noticeable lack of interest or enjoyment in activities that were once enjoyable, including hobbies, social interactions, or relationships.
- Significant Changes in Appetite or Weight – Either weight loss or weight gain (without intentional dieting), or a decrease/increase in appetite.
- Sleep Disturbances – Either insomnia (difficulty sleeping) or hypersomnia (excessive sleeping).

- Psychomotor Agitation or Retardation – Either restlessness (feeling on edge, fidgety) or slowed movement/speech, which is noticeable to others.
- Fatigue or Loss of Energy – Feeling physically and mentally drained, even after resting.
- Feelings of Worthlessness or Excessive Guilt – Intense guilt, self-blame, or feelings of being unworthy or a failure, even when there is no rational basis for it.
- Difficulty Concentrating or Indecisiveness – Trouble focusing, remembering details, or making decisions, even on small tasks.
- Recurrent Thoughts of Death or Suicide – Frequent thoughts about dying, suicidal ideation, or suicide attempts. If you are experiencing this, please reach out for immediate professional support.

Depression and resilience are deeply interconnected because resilience plays a key role in how we navigate and recover from depressive episodes, while depression can weaken the very traits that help build resilience. Understanding their relationship can help in developing strategies to manage depression and strengthen emotional endurance.

How Depression Affects Resilience

1. Reduces Emotional Strength – Depression often drains mental and emotional energy, making it harder to face everyday challenges. Tasks that once felt manageable can become overwhelming, leading to avoidance and withdrawal, which further weakens resilience.

2. Disrupts Positive Thinking and Self-Belief – Resilience relies on the ability to maintain hope, optimism, and a sense of self-efficacy (belief in one's ability to overcome obstacles). Depression distorts

these perspectives, reinforcing negative self-talk and feelings of helplessness, making setbacks feel permanent rather than temporary.

3. Weakens Motivation and Problem-Solving Skills – Resilient people actively problem-solve and seek solutions in difficult situations. Depression, however, often causes mental fog, indecisiveness, and apathy, leading to a cycle of inaction and self-doubt, which makes it harder to bounce back from difficulties.

4. Encourages Isolation Instead of Seeking Support – One of the strongest factors in resilience is having a supportive network. Depression, however, tends to make individuals withdraw from others, reducing access to emotional support, which can prolong feelings of loneliness and sadness.

How Resilience Can Help Manage Depression

Resilience doesn't mean that depression disappears, but it does help individuals better navigate depressive episodes and reduce their intensity over time. Resilience can be strengthened, allowing individuals to regain hope, confidence, and control over their mental well-being.

1. Emotional Awareness and Self-Regulation – Resilience involves recognizing emotions without judgment and developing healthy coping mechanisms. By increasing self-awareness, individuals can learn to identify depressive thoughts early and use self-regulation techniques (such as mindfulness, journaling, or therapy) to redirect negative thinking patterns.

2. Building Mental Flexibility – Resilience helps individuals reframe setbacks as learning opportunities rather than failures. This ability to shift perspective can reduce depressive thinking, making challenges feel more manageable. Cognitive Behavioral

Therapy (CBT) often incorporates reframing techniques to help develop this skill.

3. Strengthening Self-Compassion – Resilient individuals practice self-kindness rather than self-judgment. Depression often leads to harsh self-criticism, but building self-compassion can help individuals accept their struggles without feeling like they are "failing" at life. Self-compassion promotes patience, healing, and progress without pressure.

4. Encouraging Small, Actionable Steps – When resilience is low, the idea of "bouncing back" can feel overwhelming. However, resilience is built in small steps. Setting tiny, manageable goals (such as going for a short walk, reaching out to a friend, or completing a small task) creates a sense of achievement and momentum, helping to break the cycle of inaction caused by depression.

5. Fostering Connection and Seeking Support – One of the strongest factors in resilience is knowing when to reach out for help. Depression often tricks individuals into believing they should deal with things alone, but resilient people recognize the value of support. Therapy, friendships, or even small acts of social engagement can provide validation, encouragement, and perspective, which are crucial in managing depressive episodes.

Everyday Life

Depression doesn't always appear as deep sadness or crying—it can show up in subtle, everyday ways that may be overlooked. Many people with depression continue to work, go to school, and engage with others while struggling internally. Depression can be invisible, and people struggling with it often appear "fine" on the outside. Depression is not a weakness, it's a mental health condition that deserves understanding and support. Here's how depression can manifest in daily life:

1. **Physical Symptoms and Fatigue**

    - Waking up exhausted, even after a full night's sleep.
    - Feeling physically heavy or drained throughout the day.
    - Frequent headaches, muscle aches, or stomach issues with no clear cause.
    - Moving slower than usual or struggling to find the energy for basic tasks.

2. **Loss of Interest and Motivation**

    - Losing interest in hobbies or activities that once brought joy (e.g., music, art, sports, socializing).
    - Feeling like everything is monotonous, pointless, or too much effort.
    - Procrastinating on simple tasks, such as answering messages, doing laundry, or paying bills.

3. **Emotional Numbness or Irritability**

    - Instead of feeling deeply sad, some people feel emotionally "flat" or numb.
    - Increased frustration or irritability, even over small things (e.g., snapping at loved ones or coworkers).
    - Feeling disconnected from others, even in social situations.

4. **Overwhelming Negative Self-Talk**

    - Constant thoughts like "I'm not good enough," "Nothing will ever change," or "I'm a burden".

- Feeling guilty for not being "productive enough" or "happy enough".
- Replaying past mistakes or worrying excessively about the future.

5. Difficulty Focusing and Making Decisions

- Feeling mentally foggy or struggling to concentrate on work, school, or conversations.
- Simple decisions (e.g., what to eat, what to wear) feel overwhelming.
- Re-reading the same sentence or zoning out during meetings/ conversations.

6. Social Withdrawal and Isolation

- Ignoring texts, calls, or invitations because socializing feels draining.
- Feeling like people won't understand or don't want to hear about your struggles.
- Being in a room full of people but feeling completely disconnected.

7. Changes in Appetite and Sleep

- Eating too much or too little without noticing.
- Using food, alcohol, or substances to cope with emotions.
- Sleeping too much and still feeling exhausted, or struggling with insomnia.

8. Going Through the Motions

- Performing daily tasks on autopilot without feeling present (e.g., getting dressed, commuting, working, but feeling emotionally detached).

- Smiling and joking in public but feeling empty or exhausted inside ("high-functioning depression").
- Feeling like you're just existing rather than truly living.

Wearing a Mask

Living with depression often feels like putting on a mask every day, pretending to be okay while struggling internally. To the outside world, you might seem functional, even happy, but beneath the surface, there's a heavy emotional weight that's difficult to express. Many people with depression develop a habit of acting "fine" around others because they don't want to be a burden or feel like they have to explain their struggles. You might laugh at jokes, make small talk, or even post on social media, but inside, there's an overwhelming sense of emptiness, exhaustion, or sadness that no one sees.

Depression can make daily life feel like you're on autopilot. You wake up, go to work, talk to people, and do what's expected, but everything feels robotic—like you're watching your life happen rather than actually living it. Even enjoyable activities feel forced, and you might engage in them just to "keep up appearances" rather than because you genuinely feel happy. The mask of depression is often worn due to fear of judgment, fear of appearing weak, or fear that others won't understand. People might say things like, "But you don't look depressed," which can make it even harder to open up. The pressure to "hold it together" can become overwhelming, reinforcing the cycle of hiding pain instead of seeking help.

Keeping up the mask is mentally and emotionally exhausting. After a full day of pretending to be okay, you might come home and feel completely drained, needing to isolate yourself just to recover. Depression isn't just sadness—it's a constant inner battle between wanting to be understood and not wanting to be seen struggling. The more we wear the mask, the harder it becomes to take it off. If you've convinced everyone around you that you're fine, it might feel impossible to suddenly say, "Actually, I'm not okay." But taking off the mask, even just with one trusted person, can be the first step toward healing.

Breaking Free from the Mask

- Acknowledge your feelings – You don't have to fake happiness all the time. Accepting how you truly feel is the first step toward healing.
- Talk to someone you trust – Even if you don't share everything, letting someone know you're struggling can make a difference.
- Seek professional help – Therapy, support groups, or counseling can help you learn how to manage depression without feeling like you have to hide it.
- Be kind to yourself – You don't have to be perfect. Depression is not a weakness, and you deserve compassion from yourself and others.

Depression, Loneliness, and Resilience

Depression and loneliness often go hand in hand, feeding into each other in a cycle that can feel difficult to break. Depression can make you withdraw from others, increasing feelings of isolation, while loneliness can deepen depressive symptoms, making it harder to reach out for support. Resilience, however, is the key to interrupting this cycle, helping you reconnect, rebuild emotional strength, and find meaning even in difficult times.

1. **How Depression and Loneliness Reinforce Each Other**

   - Depression Leads to Withdrawal: When you're depressed, it's common to feel like you don't have the energy or motivation to engage with others. Socializing can feel overwhelming, leading to isolation.

- Loneliness Increases Negative Thinking: The more isolated you feel, the easier it is for self-doubt and negative thoughts to take over ("No one cares," "I don't belong," "I'm better off alone").

- The Cycle Repeats: The longer someone stays isolated, the harder it becomes to reconnect, making depression feel even heavier and increasing the emotional barriers to reaching out.

2. How Resilience Helps Break the Cycle

- Resilience is the ability to adapt, cope, and recover from difficult emotions, including depression and loneliness. It doesn't mean ignoring your struggles; rather, it's about learning how to navigate them in a way that fosters healing and growth. Here's how resilience can help:

- Resilience Helps You Recognize Loneliness as a Temporary Feeling: Instead of believing "I will always feel this way," resilience teaches you to see loneliness as a state that can change with small, intentional actions.

- Resilience Encourages Small Steps Toward Connection: Even if socializing feels overwhelming, resilience helps you take small, manageable steps—like sending a message, joining an online group, or stepping outside for fresh air.

- Resilience Builds Self-Compassion: Depression often comes with self-blame, but resilience encourages self-kindness, reminding you that struggling doesn't make you weak, it makes you human.

- Resilience Helps You Reframe Negative Thoughts: Instead of believing "No one wants me around," resilience encourages thoughts like "This feeling is temporary, and I can take steps to change it."

3. **Strategies for Building Resilience Against Depression and Loneliness**

- Acknowledge Your Feelings Without Judgment: Instead of suppressing loneliness or depression, acknowledge them as real, but not permanent. You are not defined by what you feel in this moment.
- Take Small Steps Toward Connection: Even if it feels difficult, try texting a friend, joining an online community, or engaging in small social activities. Human connection is essential for emotional well-being.
- Reframe Your Thoughts: When loneliness or depression tell you *"No one cares,"* challenge that thought. Ask yourself: "Is this really true, or is it my depression talking?"
- Engage in Self-Care: Even small habits like taking a walk, journaling, or practicing mindfulness can help regulate your nervous system and boost resilience.
- Seek Support When Needed: Resilience doesn't mean handling everything alone. Therapy, support groups, or even talking to a trusted friend can help you process emotions and find new coping strategies.

Overcoming Loneliness

Loneliness isn't just about being alone, it's about feeling disconnected, whether from others, yourself, or a sense of purpose. It can creep in even when surrounded by people, making it an emotional experience rather than just a physical state. Overcoming loneliness isn't about forcing social interactions; it's about rebuilding connection in ways that feel meaningful and fulfilling.

1. Reconnect with Yourself First

Loneliness often makes us feel like something is missing externally, but self-connection is the foundation for healing.

- Practice self-reflection – Journaling, meditating, or simply sitting with your thoughts can help you understand what you truly need.
- Engage in activities you enjoy – Even solo activities (reading, exercising, cooking, painting) help create a sense of fulfillment and self-worth.
- Be kind to yourself – Replace self-judgment ("I'm alone because something is wrong with me") with self-compassion ("I deserve connection, and I can take steps to build it").

2. Shift the Focus from Quantity to Quality in Relationships

Loneliness isn't just about having people around, it's about feeling seen, valued, and understood.

- Reach out to a trusted friend or family member – Even a small text or call can break the cycle of isolation.
- Deepen existing connections – Instead of focusing on expanding your social circle, nurture meaningful conversations with those already in your life.
- Join a community with shared interests – Whether it's a support group, online forum, hobby club, or fitness class, shared experiences foster connection.

3. Take Small, Intentional Social Steps

When loneliness is overwhelming, socializing can feel exhausting, but small, low-pressure interactions can help rebuild confidence.

- Start with small interactions – A simple smile, greeting a neighbor, or casual conversation with a coworker can spark a sense of connection.
- Volunteer or help others – Giving back not only provides a sense of purpose, but it also creates natural social connections.
- Adopt a pet – If possible, pets provide companionship and emotional comfort, helping to ease loneliness.

4. Challenge Negative Thought Patterns About Loneliness

Loneliness often comes with self-defeating thoughts, making it feel impossible to change.

- Reframe your thoughts – Instead of "No one cares," shift to "I haven't connected with the right people yet."
- Understand that loneliness is a feeling, not a fact – Your mind might tell you "I'm always alone," but feelings are temporary, and connection is always possible.

Depression, Heartbreak, and Resilience

Heartbreak and depression are deeply intertwined, as the pain of losing a relationship, whether romantic, friendship, or family, can trigger feelings of deep sadness, loneliness, and even a loss of self-identity. When heartbreak is intense or prolonged, it can lead to depressive symptoms, making it harder to move forward. However, resilience is the bridge between pain and healing, helping individuals regain emotional strength and find meaning beyond their loss.

1. How Heartbreak Can Lead to Depression

Heartbreak is more than just emotional pain—it can physically and neurologically affect the brain. Studies show that romantic rejection activates the same brain regions associated with physical pain. This can lead to:

- Emotional exhaustion and numbness – The brain struggles to process the loss, making daily activities feel meaningless.
- Obsessive thinking and rumination – Replaying the past relationship, wondering "What went wrong?" or "What could I have done differently?"
- Social withdrawal – Avoiding people due to shame, sadness, or the fear of judgment.
- Loss of self-worth – Feeling "If I were enough, they wouldn't have left," leading to self-doubt and insecurity.

2. How Resilience Helps Heal Heartbreak and Depression

Resilience doesn't mean avoiding pain—it means learning how to move through it without losing yourself. Heartbreak and depression don't have to define you; resilience helps you grow from them.

- Emotional regulation – Resilient people allow themselves to feel and process emotions without suppressing them. Instead of avoiding pain, they sit with it, knowing that healing comes through acknowledgment, not avoidance.
- Rebuilding self-worth – After heartbreak, it's easy to base self-value on external validation. Resilience helps shift focus inward, recognizing that your worth is not determined by someone else's decision to stay or leave.
- Shifting perspective – Instead of seeing heartbreak as an ending, resilient individuals view it as redirection—an opportunity for self-growth, stronger relationships, and new experiences.
- Taking small steps forward – Resilience is built through action. Whether it's journaling, therapy, reconnecting with friends, or

rediscovering hobbies, small steps help regain confidence and emotional strength.

3. **Strategies for Building Resilience Through Heartbreak and Depression**

1. Acknowledge the Pain, but Don't Let It Consume You

   - Allow yourself to grieve the loss without judgment. Cry if you need to, express your feelings, but remind yourself: This is a chapter, not the whole story.

2. Challenge Negative Self-Talk

   - If heartbreak leads to self-blame ("I wasn't good enough"), reframe it: "This relationship ending does not define my worth."

3. Reconnect with Yourself

   - Sometimes, relationships consume our identity. Use this time to rediscover what makes you happy, outside of another person.

4. Surround Yourself with Support

   - Lean on friends, family, or even a therapist. Isolation prolongs depression, while connection speeds healing.

5. Find Purpose Beyond the Pain

   - Heartbreak can be a reset button. What have you always wanted to do for yourself? Travel, start a new hobby, set new goals? Turn pain into purpose.

Depression, Grief, and Resilience

Grief and depression are often intertwined, as both involve deep emotional pain, sadness, and a sense of loss. While grief is a natural response to losing someone or something important, depression can develop when the pain becomes overwhelming, persistent, or interferes with daily life. Resilience is what helps us process grief without being consumed by it, allowing us to heal while carrying our loss forward in a way that honors what we've lost without losing ourselves. Grief changes you, but it doesn't mean you are broken. Depression may try to convince you that you'll never feel joy again, but resilience proves otherwise. Healing doesn't mean forgetting, it means finding a way to live, love, and grow while carrying your loss with you in a way that honors its meaning without losing yourself.

1. The Difference Between Grief and Depression

While grief and depression share similar emotional experiences, they are not the same:

- Grief is an emotional response to loss—whether it's the death of a loved one, the end of a relationship, or the loss of a life chapter. It often comes in waves and includes sadness, longing, and sometimes even moments of joy when remembering what was lost.
- Depression is a persistent emotional state that can develop when grief becomes overwhelming. Unlike grief, which fluctuates, depression often brings a constant sense of emptiness, hopelessness, and detachment from life.

Signs grief may be turning into depression:

- Persistent sadness and hopelessness that doesn't ease over time.

- Loss of interest in daily activities or feeling numb for weeks or months.
- Intense self-blame or guilt over the loss.
- Social withdrawal and isolation beyond what feels natural for grieving.
- Thoughts of worthlessness or suicidal ideation.

2. How Resilience Helps Us Move Through Grief and Depression

Resilience doesn't mean avoiding grief or "moving on" quickly, it means learning to carry loss without letting it define or destroy you. It allows you to hold onto love and memories while still finding a way forward.

- Resilience allows space for grief -Instead of pushing emotions away, resilient people allow themselves to feel grief fully, knowing that emotions come and go in waves. Suppressing pain can lead to depression, but accepting and expressing it leads to healing.
- Resilience helps reframe loss -While grief often feels like losing a part of yourself, resilience helps shift the perspective: "I will always love and miss this, but I can still find meaning in life."
- Resilience Builds Emotional Strength Over Time - Initially, everything feels unbearable, but resilience reminds us that pain lessens as we learn to cope. It doesn't erase loss, but it teaches us how to live with it.
- Resilience Encourages Connection -Grief and depression can make you want to withdraw, but resilience reminds you that healing happens through connection, whether with friends, family, support groups, or spiritual practices.

3. **Strategies for Building Resilience Through Grief and Depression**

a) Allow Yourself to Mourn Without Judgment

- Healing isn't about "getting over it." Let yourself feel the pain, sadness, and love without guilt or pressure.

b) Find Ways to Honor the Loss

- Writing letters, creating memory keepsakes, or engaging in meaningful rituals can help process emotions and keep connections alive in a healthy way.

c) Challenge the Isolation That Comes with Depression

- Even when you don't feel like it, try to stay connected to at least one person, someone who listens without judgment.

d) Rebuild Routine and Purpose Slowly

- Depression and grief can make life feel empty. Start small, simple daily goals, walks, creative activities, to restore meaning and engagement.

e) Seek Professional Support If Needed

- Therapy, support groups, or grief counseling can help when emotions feel unbearable. You don't have to carry this alone.

CHAPTER 6

Resilience and Trauma

Trauma is a heavy and complex subject, and there is no way to fully cover its depth in just one chapter. Trauma affects people in different ways, shaping how they see themselves, others, and the world around them. It influences thought patterns, emotional responses, and even physical health, making it a deeply personal and layered experience. Rather than attempting to tackle every aspect of trauma at once, I want to focus on key elements that can help in understanding its impact and, most importantly, how to move forward. This chapter will not be an exhaustive discussion, but rather a starting point, a foundation for recognizing trauma's effects and exploring paths toward healing and resilience. Because trauma is not a one-size-fits-all experience, healing is also unique for each person. Healing may include therapy, structured support, self-reflection, healthy and supportive relationships, or creative expression. No matter the journey, the goal is not to erase trauma but to reclaim control over how it shapes your life moving forward.

I want to focus on key elements that can help in understanding trauma's impact and how it shapes a person's emotions, thoughts, and behaviors. Trauma doesn't just live in the past, it affects the present and future, influencing how we respond to stress, relationships, and even our sense of self.

1. Emotional and Psychological Impact – Trauma can alter self-perception, increase anxiety or depression, and create patterns

of hypervigilance, avoidance, or emotional numbness. Recognizing these effects is the first step toward healing.

2. <u>How Trauma Affects Relationships</u> – Many people with trauma struggle with trust, vulnerability, or emotional regulation in relationships. Understanding these challenges can help foster self-awareness and healthier connections.

3. <u>Breaking Cycles of Trauma</u> – Trauma often leads to repetitive patterns of thinking and behavior that feel inescapable. Learning how to interrupt these cycles is a powerful part of resilience and growth.

4. <u>Pathways to Healing</u> – Healing from trauma isn't about erasing the past but about reclaiming control over how it shapes your future. Exploring tools such as therapy, mindfulness, self-compassion, and support systems can help build a strong foundation for resilience.

Trauma and Resilience

Trauma has the power to break a person down, but resilience is what allows them to rebuild. Trauma can shake our sense of safety, identity, and trust, making it feel as though the world is unpredictable, and we are powerless. However, resilience is the ability to adapt, heal, and regain control after experiencing adversity. It doesn't mean forgetting or pretending trauma didn't happen, it means learning to move forward without being defined by it.

1. How Trauma Impacts Resilience

Trauma can weaken resilience by:

- Overwhelming the nervous system – The brain remains stuck in survival mode (fight, flight, freeze, or fawn), making it hard to process emotions or feel safe.

- Shaping negative self-beliefs – Trauma often leads to thoughts like "I am not safe," "I am not good enough," or "I have no control." These beliefs make it harder to recover.
- Creating avoidance patterns – To protect themselves from pain, people may avoid relationships, emotions, or situations that remind them of their trauma, limiting their ability to heal.

2. How Resilience Helps Heal Trauma

Resilience doesn't erase trauma, but it helps reshape the way we respond to it. Building resilience after trauma includes:

- Regaining a sense of safety – Teaching the nervous system that not every moment is a threat helps create stability. Practices like mindfulness, deep breathing, and grounding techniques can help.
- Challenging negative thought patterns – Resilient individuals learn to rewrite the internal dialogue left by trauma, replacing self-doubt with self-compassion and self-trust.
- Reconnecting with others – Trauma often isolates people, but resilience grows in safe, supportive relationships that provide encouragement and healing.
- Finding meaning beyond the pain – Many resilient people use their trauma as a source of strength, whether through personal growth, advocacy, or helping others who have experienced similar pain.

3. Practical Ways to Build Resilience After Trauma

1. Acknowledge and Process the Trauma – Healing starts with accepting and understanding what happened, rather than suppressing it. Therapy, journaling, or talking to a trusted person can help.

2. Strengthen Emotional Regulation – Learning how to calm overwhelming emotions through breathing exercises, movement, or creative outlets can help regain control.

3. Challenge Limiting Beliefs – Instead of "I will never heal," shift to "Healing takes time, and I am working toward it."

4. Engage in Restorative Activities – Yoga, nature walks, music, or art can help reconnect the mind and body, counteracting trauma's effects.

5. Seek Support When Needed – Healing doesn't have to be done alone. Finding therapy, support groups, or trusted friends can make a significant difference.

CHAPTER 7

Additional tips for managing resilience barriers

Positive Toxicity

Positivity is an important component of mental wellness, but when misapplied, it can become toxic positivity, the idea that we should always maintain a happy, optimistic attitude regardless of reality. While positive thinking is a powerful tool, it should be practiced with realism and emotional honesty. True positivity is not about ignoring struggles, suppressing emotions, or pretending everything is fine, it's about adopting a healthy, balanced perspective on the truth while still allowing space for difficult emotions.

Toxic positivity occurs when positivity is forced in a way that dismisses, invalidates, or minimizes real struggles. It can sound like:

> "Just stay positive!"
> "Everything happens for a reason."
> "It could be worse, so stop complaining."
> "Good vibes only!"

While these statements may seem well-intended, they often shut down genuine emotions rather than allowing space for processing challenges. When people feel pressured to always be positive, they may:

- Suppress real emotions like sadness, frustration, or grief.
- Feel guilty or shameful for experiencing negative emotions.
- Avoid addressing difficult situations, leading to unresolved issues.

Positivity should not be about denying reality, but rather about choosing a productive, growth-oriented response to challenges. Healthy positivity acknowledges that:

- Life includes struggles, and it's okay to feel emotions fully.
- Difficult emotions serve a purpose, helping us grow, learn, and heal.
- A positive mindset is a tool, not an escape, and it should be paired with action and self-awareness.

Realistic positivity says:

> "This situation is hard, but I will get through it."
> "I'm struggling, and that's okay. I can work through this at my own pace."
> "I acknowledge my pain while also believing in my ability to heal."
> "I can hold both sadness and hope at the same time."

You don't have to be happy all the time. Give yourself permission to feel sadness, anger, frustration, or grief without guilt. These emotions deserve space just as much as joy does. Positivity should support emotional resilience, not dismiss real struggles. It should encourage hope, problem-solving, and self-compassion rather than avoidance or suppression. Positivity is a tool, not an escape.

Instead of forcing fake positivity, practice perspective-shifting:

"This is fine, everything happens for a reason."
(shifts to)
"This is difficult, but I am capable of handling it."

Nutrient Deficiencies

Resilience isn't just about mental strength; it's also deeply connected to physical health. Our bodies and minds work together, meaning that when we are deficient in essential nutrients or struggling with chronic health conditions, our ability to handle stress, regulate emotions, and maintain energy for daily challenges is compromised. It is always a good idea to stay diligent about your health, including keeping up with physicals, yearly checks-ups, and lab work. You can not "out cope" nutrient deficiencies, these must be handled with the appropriate physical or medical care. Being deficient in essential vitamins and minerals, such as B vitamins, vitamin D, magnesium, and iron (anemia), can lead to fatigue, brain fog, and mood imbalances.

Anemia is linked to low mood, anxiety, and even depression, which can weaken emotional resilience. Low levels of vitamin D have been associated with increased risk of depression and fatigue, making it harder to stay optimistic and cope with stress. Low B12 levels can cause memory issues, depression, and nerve problems, reducing focus and resilience. Magnesium helps relax the nervous system. Low levels contribute to stress, muscle tension, and sleep disturbances, making it harder to recover from emotional or physical stress. The thyroid gland regulates metabolism, energy, and hormone balance. If your thyroid is underactive (hypothyroidism) or overactive (hyperthyroidism), it can severely impact mental health and resilience leading to fatigue, depression, brain fog, weight gain, and difficulty coping with stress, anxiety, irritability, rapid heartbeat, and sleep disturbances. High blood pressure (hypertension) puts extra strain on the heart and brain, impacting mental clarity, mood regulation, and stress response. Blood sugar fluctuations affect brain function, emotional stability, and stress resilience.

CHAPTER 8

Conquering Emotional Intrusions

Emotional intrusions, those unwanted, repetitive thoughts and feelings that disrupt your sense of peace, can feel overwhelming, as if they control your mind rather than the other way around. They come in the form of self-doubt, anxiety, past regrets, or fears about the future, often hijacking your emotions and dictating your reactions. They become background noise in daily life. However, the moment you learn to conquer these intrusions, something powerful happens, you experience the joy of mental freedom, self-trust, and emotional strength, which is what this book is all about.

The Turning Point: Gaining Control Over Emotional Intrusions

The joy of conquering emotional intrusions comes from learning that you are not your thoughts or emotions, you are the observer of them. You begin to realize that:

- You don't have to believe everything your mind tells you. Thoughts are just thoughts, not facts.
- You can choose how to respond rather than react impulsively to emotional triggers.
- You are stronger than the emotions trying to control you.

The Joy of Breaking Free

When you start conquering emotional intrusions, life feels lighter, clearer, and more peaceful. Some of the joys include:

- Mental Clarity - You no longer feel consumed by racing thoughts and endless worries. Your mind becomes a space for problem-solving and creativity, rather than fear and doubt.
- Emotional Stability - Instead of being overwhelmed by emotions, you learn to process them without letting them define you.
- Greater Self-Trust - You stop second-guessing yourself and start believing in your own judgment and strength.
- A Sense of Freedom - Without emotional intrusions controlling you, you feel free to live, take risks, and embrace joy without fear.

How to Conquer Emotional Intrusions and Reclaim Joy

1. Recognize the Intrusion Without Judgment

- Instead of reacting emotionally, pause and observe the thought or feeling. "This is an anxious thought, but it is not me."

2. Challenge and Reframe Negative Thoughts

- If an intrusive thought says "I'm not good enough," challenge it: "That's just my fear talking. I am capable and strong."

3. Use Grounding Techniques

- Breathe deeply, focus on your surroundings, or engage in a physical activity to break the cycle of intrusive thoughts.

4. Strengthen Your Resilience Through Action

- Each time you face emotional discomfort instead of avoiding it, you train your brain to handle future challenges with more confidence.

5. **Celebrate Your Progress**

    - Conquering emotional intrusions isn't about eliminating them completely, it's about learning how to not let them control you. Every time you redirect a negative thought or choose peace over panic, you acknowledge your growth.

Journal prompts for celebrating your progress:

1. **What's one moment in the past week or month where you handled a challenge in a way you're proud of?**

    - Reflect on a specific situation where you successfully managed stress, overcame a fear, or handled an emotional challenge. Celebrate how you approached it with strength and resilience.

2. **What positive habits or practices have you developed that are making a difference in your daily life?**

    - Think about the small changes you've made—whether it's a new morning routine, regular self-care, or setting healthier boundaries—and how they've impacted your mental, emotional, or physical well-being.

3. **What's a limiting belief or fear you've let go of, and how has that shift changed your outlook?**

    - Reflect on any negative thoughts or fears that once held you back, and how you've learned to challenge or release them. How has this change empowered you to take action or feel more confident?

4. **What are three things you've learned about yourself through recent challenges or setbacks?**

- Every experience, even the tough ones, offers insight. Write about the lessons you've gained, how you've grown, and how those lessons are shaping you into a stronger, more resilient person.

5. How can you acknowledge and celebrate your progress, even if it feels small?

- Often, progress feels subtle. Reflect on the steps you've taken, no matter how small they seem, and think about ways to celebrate them. How can you give yourself credit for the hard work you've put in so far?

A recap of the skills sprinkled throughout this book:

1. Self-Awareness

Self-awareness is the foundation of emotional health. It involves recognizing your feelings, thoughts, and behaviors, and understanding how they impact you and those around you. This skill allows you to respond to situations mindfully rather than react impulsively.

- **Recognizing Emotions**: Being able to identify and label what you're feeling helps you understand the root causes of your emotions. This insight allows you to address feelings in a healthy way. It's a first step toward emotional regulation, as you can't manage emotions you don't understand.
- **Tracking Negative Thought Patterns**: Understanding how your thoughts influence your emotions and behaviors can break unhelpful cycles. Journaling, mindfulness, or therapy can help you track negative thoughts like catastrophizing or black-and-white thinking, which often fuel anxiety or depression.

- **Mindfulness**: Practicing mindfulness involves being **fully present** in each moment and observing your thoughts and emotions without judgment. It helps you become more aware of your internal world, reducing reactivity and increasing emotional clarity.

2. Emotional Regulation

Emotional regulation is the ability to manage and respond to emotional experiences in a way that is balanced and adaptive. This skill prevents emotions from overwhelming you and allows you to maintain stability, even during stressful times.

- **Breathing Exercises**: Techniques like diaphragmatic breathing (deep belly breathing) or box breathing (inhale for 4, hold for 4, exhale for 4) activate the parasympathetic nervous system, which helps calm the body's stress response. This is particularly helpful in moments of panic, anxiety, or overwhelm.
- **Grounding Techniques**: Grounding exercises, such as the 5-4-3-2-1 technique, help bring attention back to the present moment. Identify 5 things you see, 4 things you feel, 3 things you hear, 2 things you smell, and 1 thing you taste to stay present. These exercises anchor your body and mind, providing immediate relief from intense emotions and anxiety.
- **Self-Soothing:** Self-soothing involves comforting yourself in ways that reduce distress. This could include gentle touch (like hand on heart), listening to calming music, engaging in a warm bath, or taking a walk. These actions signal the brain that it's safe to relax.

3. Self-Compassion and Self-Forgiveness

Self-compassion involves treating yourself with kindness rather than criticism, especially during difficult times. Self-forgiveness is crucial for letting go of past mistakes, releasing guilt, and moving forward with a sense of peace.

- **Practicing Self-Compassion**: Instead of internalizing failure or stress, self-compassion involves talking to yourself with kindness and recognizing that everyone experiences struggles. Being gentle with yourself is vital for emotional healing.
- **Forgiving Yourself**: Self-forgiveness isn't about excusing mistakes; it's about accepting your imperfection and allowing yourself to **learn and grow** from experiences without being burdened by shame or guilt.

4. Building Resilience

Resilience is the ability to bounce back from setbacks and adapt in the face of adversity. It's about-facing challenges with strength and flexibility, rather than being overwhelmed by them.

- **Facing Discomfort**: Rather than avoiding difficult emotions or experiences, resilient people face them head-on. They recognize that discomfort is part of life and that it's temporary. By facing discomfort, we build emotional strength.
- **Problem-Solving**: Resilience includes the ability to find solutions in challenging circumstances. Instead of feeling stuck, resilient people assess situations, make decisions, and adapt their strategies. This gives them a sense of agency, even in adversity.
- **Adopting a Growth Mindset**: A growth mindset helps you see setbacks as opportunities for growth, not as failures. Instead of thinking, "I'll never get through this," resilient individuals think, "I can handle this, and I will learn from it."
- **Setting Small, Achievable Goals**: Resilience is built one step at a time. Breaking large tasks into smaller, manageable pieces helps

you maintain momentum and feel a sense of accomplishment along the way, even when things feel overwhelming.

5. Cognitive Behavioral Skills

These skills help you reframe negative thoughts and change unhelpful behavior patterns that can fuel anxiety, depression, or stress. Cognitive-behavioral skills promote healthy thinking, which leads to healthier emotional responses.

- **Reframing Negative Self-Talk**: When intrusive or self-critical thoughts arise, resilience comes from challenging and replacing them. If you think, "I'm not good enough," reframing would involve recognizing this thought as an exaggeration and replacing it with a more balanced perspective like "I am enough, and I am capable of growth."
- **Self-Talk Awareness**: Becoming aware of the **tone and content** of your inner dialogue is key to managing emotions. The more you practice identifying negative self-talk, the easier it becomes to **reframe** it toward more supportive, positive language.

6. Mindfulness and Grounding

Mindfulness and grounding are both critical tools for staying present in the moment and interrupting overwhelming emotions. These techniques reduce anxiety and prevent your mind from spiraling into past regrets or future worries.

- **Mindfulness Techniques**: Practicing mindfulness involves engaging in activities like meditation, breathing exercises, or body scans that allow you to observe your thoughts without being attached to them. It promotes awareness of the present moment, which can be deeply calming and grounding.

- **Present-Moment Awareness**: Being fully engaged with your environment and emotions helps stop the cycle of rumination or worry. Focusing on your senses (what you see, hear, smell, taste, and feel) can shift your attention away from negative thinking.

7. Connection and Seeking Support

Support from others plays a vital role in mental health. Building strong, healthy relationships and seeking help when needed are essential for growth and healing.

- **Building and Nurturing Relationships**: Emotional connection fosters healing. Spending time with loved ones and cultivating meaningful relationships is vital for resilience.
- **Seeking Professional Help**: Sometimes, self-help strategies aren't enough, and professional help is necessary. A therapist or counselor can offer insights and tools that help you process trauma or manage mental health challenges.
- **Sharing Vulnerabilities**: Opening up to trusted people can reduce isolation and increase connection. Vulnerability is not weakness—it's a strength that allows for emotional support and healing.

8. Positive Reinforcement and Self-Motivation

Positive reinforcement encourages you to continue engaging in healthy behaviors, and self-motivation keeps you moving forward despite setbacks.

- **Rewarding Progress**: Celebrating small victories encourages consistency and progress. Whether it's acknowledging a completed task or recognizing emotional growth, positive reinforcement keeps you motivated.

- **Using Positive Reinforcement**: Encourage healthy behaviors—like reaching out for support or practicing self-care—by recognizing the positive impact they have on your well-being.

9. Creating an Emotionally Safe Space

An internal safety zone helps you find stability in moments of emotional chaos, creating a space where you can feel secure and calm no matter what's happening outside.

- **Creating an Internal Safety Zone**: Developing mental tools, like visualization or grounding exercises, helps you feel safe and centered when external stressors arise.
- **Visualizing a Safe Space**: Imagining a comforting environment, whether real or imagined, allows you to access inner peace when needed.
- **Strengthening Your Sense of Control**: Recognizing that you have control over your responses helps regain a sense of safety. Setting boundaries and practicing self-advocacy can also help build emotional security.

These mental health skills are not isolated—they work together to build emotional resilience, self-awareness, and stability. Mastering these skills allows you to navigate stress, trauma, and emotional discomfort with greater ease, confidence, and strength. It's a journey of learning how to manage emotions and foster a balanced, healthier mindset, empowering you to face life's challenges with compassion and clarity.

Self-Care Resiliency Plan

This Self-Care Resiliency Plan is not about perfection, but about commitment. A commitment to choosing yourself, repeatedly, even on the hardest days. A promise that you will nurture yourself through all seasons of life.

I. Cultivating Self-Awareness

Affirmation: "I will become more aware of my thoughts, emotions, and behaviors so that I can respond rather than react."

Daily Practices for Self-Awareness:

- Check in with yourself: What am I feeling right now? What thoughts are running through my mind?
- Keep a journal: Track recurring thoughts, emotions, and behaviors. Look for patterns that influence your mood.
- Practice mindfulness: Take 5-10 minutes each day to sit in stillness, focus on your breath, and observe your thoughts without judgment.
- Use a self-awareness mantra: "I allow myself to feel, and I trust myself to handle my emotions."

II. Emotional Regulation & Grounding Techniques

Affirmation: "I will regulate my emotions by responding with patience and self-care, not avoidance or self-judgment."

Tools for Calming the Nervous System:

- Deep breathing exercises to reset stress responses.

- 5-4-3-2-1 grounding technique: Identify 5 things you see, 4 things you feel, 3 things you hear, 2 things you smell, and 1 thing you taste to stay present.
- Progressive muscle relaxation to release stored tension in the body.
- Movement-based regulation: Engage in stretching, walking, or yoga to discharge stress from the body.
- Self-soothing techniques: Hold a warm cup of tea, wrap yourself in a blanket, or practice self-hugging to promote feelings of comfort and safety.

III. Practicing Self-Compassion and Self-Forgiveness

Affirmation: "I will treat myself with kindness and allow myself to be human."

Daily Practices for Self-Compassion:

- Rewrite negative self-talk: Challenge self-criticism and reframe it into supportive, realistic affirmations.
- Use self-compassionate language: Instead of "I should be stronger," say "I am doing the best I can, and that is enough."
- Write a letter to yourself: Express kindness toward yourself, acknowledging your struggles and reminding yourself of your worth.
- Forgive yourself for past mistakes: Say "I release the past. I choose to move forward with grace."

IV. Strengthening Resilience Through Small, Intentional Steps

Affirmation: "I will build my resilience one step at a time, knowing that healing is a journey."

Resilience-Building Actions:

- Set small, achievable goals: Break overwhelming tasks into manageable steps. Progress, no matter how small, builds confidence.
- Embrace discomfort as growth: Remind yourself that challenges help you evolve rather than define you.
- Adopt a growth mindset: Instead of "I can't handle this," shift to "This is difficult, but I am learning and growing through it."
- Celebrate small wins: Recognize every step forward, even if it's simply getting out of bed on a tough day.

V. Cognitive Reframing: Shifting Limiting Beliefs

Affirmation: "I will challenge the stories I tell myself that no longer serve me."

Reframing Negative Thoughts:

- Recognize automatic negative thoughts: Are they based on fact or fear?
- Challenge limiting beliefs: Replace "I am not good enough" with "I am constantly learning and growing."
- Use positive self-affirmations: Write down and repeat affirmations daily, such as "I am worthy of love, success, and peace."

VI. Connection and Seeking Support

Affirmation: "I will not isolate myself in struggle. I will allow myself to seek support when needed."

Ways to Build Emotional Connection:

- Reach out to someone you trust: A friend, family member, mentor, or therapist.
- Engage in community: Join a support group, hobby class, or online forum that aligns with your interests.
- Practice vulnerability: Share your struggles and joys with those who support you.
- Set healthy boundaries: Choose relationships that nourish you and limit exposure to toxic interactions.

VII. Creating an Internal Safety Zone

Affirmation: "I will build a place within myself where I feel safe, no matter what happens externally."

How to Create a Mental & Emotional Safe Space:

- Visualize a comforting place: A memory, imaginary location, or peaceful setting where you feel safe.
- Use grounding objects: Carry a small item (like a stone or bracelet) that reminds you of stability.
- Repeat a safety mantra: "I am safe. I am in control. I am at peace."

VIII. Cultivating Joy and Gratitude

Affirmation: "I will actively seek moments of joy, even in the midst of struggle."

<u>Daily Joy Practices:</u>

- List three things you're grateful for each day.
- Engage in activities that bring joy—painting, music, writing, dancing, or nature walks.
- Laugh often: Watch a funny video, call a friend, or do something playful.

IX. Writing Your Own Love Letter to Yourself

<u>Affirmation</u>: "I will celebrate the love I have for myself, honoring every step of my journey."

<u>Write a Personal Love Letter to Yourself:</u>

- Start with kindness: "Dear [Your Name], I see you. I honor your strength and growth."
- Acknowledge your progress: Reflect on how you've grown, healed, and evolved.
- Offer encouragement: Remind yourself that you are capable, strong, and worthy of love.
- End with a commitment: "I promise to keep showing up for myself with love and patience."

X. Make a Commitment to Your Physical Health

<u>Affirmation</u>: "I honor my body by nourishing it, moving it, and resting it with love."

Remember, your physical health plays a crucial role in your ability to be resilient. When you nourish your body with proper food, movement, and rest, you build the strength and energy needed to navigate life's challenges with clarity and confidence. Taking care of yourself physically is not just about wellness, it's about equipping yourself with the endurance, stability, and vitality to bounce back from setbacks and thrive in every aspect of life. For evolutionary resilience, physical health and mental health go hand and hand.

Common Checklist to Help Monitor Your Physical Health: these are only suggestions as you will create your own health plan tailored just for you.

- Keep up with regular checkups and doctor appointments.
- Know the status of your numbers such as the information you would receive from lab work (i.e. iron, vitamin deficiencies, cholesterol, glucose, thyroid, blood pressure, etc).
- Drink water to avoid dehydration.
- Exercise regularly, and try to have fun with it.
- Eat a healthy and balanced diet.
- Create a consistent morning and night routine for restful sleep.
- Create a plan to care for your skin, teeth, and eyes for optimal functioning.
- Be intentional with relaxation throughout the day.

XI. Reflection & Commitment to Growth

Affirmation: "I am my own safe space. I am evolving. I am resilient."

How to Maintain Your Self-Care Resiliency Plan:

- Check in weekly: Reflect on what's working and where adjustments are needed.
- Be flexible: Healing is not linear. Allow yourself grace to adapt your plan as needed.
- Celebrate your progress: Even when small, every step matters.

My Final Thoughts....

Thinking of evolutionary resilience as a love letter to yourself is a beautiful way to imagine personal growth and emotional strength. It transforms resilience from a concept about endurance or simply surviving hardship, into something much more meaningful, a gentle, loving acknowledgment of your inner strength and the way you evolve through life's challenges. Just like a love letter, it is a celebration of who you are, embracing both the light and the dark, the strength and the vulnerability, and the continuous process of becoming a better version of yourself.

A love letter to yourself doesn't shy away from difficult moments or painful experiences. It acknowledges and accepts all parts of your journey, even the hard parts. Rather than dismissing setbacks or mistakes, it honors the lessons they've brought, and how they've contributed to your growth. Just as a love letter expresses admiration for all someone is—flaws and all—this mindset invites you to see yourself through the same compassionate, non-judgmental lens. It says: "Everything I've experienced has shaped me into the resilient person I am today."

A love letter to yourself is also a reminder of your inner strength. It's about seeing the resilience you've built, sometimes without even realizing it. Every time you bounce back from hardship, every time you learn to cope, you're showing evolutionary resilience, a kind of strength that doesn't just help you survive, but thrive and adapt. Resilience isn't about "bouncing back to who you were," it's about evolving, becoming more attuned to your emotions, your needs, and your growth. The letter to yourself would recognize and celebrate these moments of growth and transformation.

A love letter is written with deep compassion, and this is essential in the context of resilience. It's not about pressuring yourself to constantly be "strong," but instead, it's about recognizing that resilience requires periods of rest, self-compassion, and understanding. Sometimes, resilience means giving yourself permission to feel, rest, or step back, rather than forcing yourself to keep pushing forward. A love letter to yourself would acknowledge the need for gentle self-care and affirm that you are enough, even when you don't feel like you're at your best.

A love letter isn't just a reflection of the past; it's a commitment to the future. Evolutionary resilience involves looking ahead, knowing that there will be more challenges—but also knowing that you have everything you need to handle them. The love letter would encourage you to approach life with hope and empowerment, knowing that no matter what comes your way, you are capable of facing it with the same courage and grace that you have in the past.

A love letter to yourself also has an underlying tone of gratitude, for where you've been and how far you've come. Resilience grows when you recognize that even in difficult times, there are opportunities for growth. Gratitude helps shift your focus from what's lacking to what's abundant, including the inner strength you've developed along the way. A love letter acknowledges the gift of resilience, understanding that each challenge brings the possibility of transformation and empowerment.

Finally, a love letter acknowledges and celebrates who you are now, in this moment, knowing that you are constantly evolving. Your resilience is a reflection of your uniqueness, and every hardship, every triumph, and every emotional experience adds to the person you are today. It's about embracing who you are now while recognizing that you're always growing, always changing, and always becoming more aligned with the best version of yourself.

It's the strength in your bones
It's the twinkle in your eyes
You're coming alive like a blossomed cherry
You are evolutionary

-Prudence Hatchett

About the Author

Prudence Hatchett earned a BA in Psychology (2004) and an M.S. in Special Education with a concentration in Emotional Disability (2006) from Mississippi State University. She earned an M.Ed. in Counselor Education (2015) and completed the master level Emotional Disability Endorsement Program in Education (2017) from the University of Mississippi. She is a National Certified Counselor (NCC), Licensed Professional Counselor (LPC) & Board Qualified Supervisor (LPC-S), Board Certified Telemental Health Provider (BC-TMH), Certified Clinical Anxiety Treatment Professional (CCATP), Certified Grief Professional (CGP), Advanced Certified Autism Specialist (ACAS), Certified Addictions-Informed Mental Health Professional (CAIMHP), Certified Employee Assistance Professional (CEAP), US DOT Substance Abuse Professional (SAP), and a Board Certified Coach (BCC). She was named a Subject Matter Expert (SME) for the Center for Credentialing & Education. Prudence opened her own private practice, PH Counseling, LLC in 2018, which provides a variety of services including counseling, coaching, consultations, clinical supervision, and education. She holds a Master's level AA educator's license, with educational endorsements in the areas of Guidance Counseling, Mild/Moderate Disabilities, Emotional Disability, and Psychology. Prudence has over 18 years of combined experience in the mental health and education fields of practice. Along with being an expert speaker, Prudence is also a best-selling author and co-author with journals and books available for purchase at major retailers such as Amazon, Walmart, Barnes & Noble, and Books-A-Million. Prudence created her brand and ecommerce store, "Learn with Prudence," which she aims to increase education for building mental health wellness and increasing confidence towards sustainable behavior change. Her digital store is equipped with an array of different products such as digital eBooks, fillable workbooks, and her custom designed novelties. She supports people in maturing their mental health and emotional wellness through the power of education, strength exploration, skill building, and elevating confidence. She leads people towards understanding their own thought patterns to reverse negative processing to experience greater fulfillment and happiness. Prudence is excited to share her message of empowerment and transformation towards becoming the healthiest version of the truest self.

PH Counseling, LLC
https://www.phcounseling.org
Learn with Prudence
https://learn-with-prudence.myshopify.com/

Evolutionary Resilience
The Program

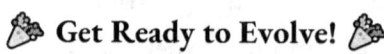 Get Ready to Evolve!

Introducing **"Evolutionary Resilience"** your new go-to program for leveling up your emotional strength and finally breaking free from the cycles of anxiety, depression, and emotional overwhelm! ✸

This isn't just another self-help course; it's a full-on mind-body-soul transformation. Inside the program, you'll get powerful video lessons, guided exercises, practical tools, journal prompts, and my personal style of real talk and authenticity that walks you through every step of building unstoppable resilience.

✨ You'll learn how to:

- Calm your nervous system and quiet intrusive thoughts
- Build self-trust and bounce back from setbacks
- Handle emotions without drowning in them
- Break unhealthy patterns and create healthier ones
- Feel stronger, more centered, and in control of your life

Whether you're just starting your healing journey or ready to take things to the next level, Evolutionary Resilience gives you the structure, support, and strategy to make real change sustainable.

💡 Why *Evolutionary Resilience* is Different

This program was designed with heart and backed by years of professional experience. As a versatile professional in the education and mental wellness space, I've taken everything I've learned from working with real people facing real struggles and packed it into a transformational experience. This isn't about pretending everything's okay. It's about giving you the emotional tools, scientific understanding, and daily practices you need to feel true resilience.

💪 It's time to evolve into the version of you that thrives, not just survives.

🔥 Are you ready to conquer your emotional intrusions and finally feel free?

👉 Visit my website, **www.phcounseling.org,** to learn more about the program.

This is your safe space. Your launch pad. Your comeback story in motion.

Together, let's rewrite what your story looks like, resiliently and unapologetically!

www.ingramcontent.com/pod-product-compliance
Lightning Source LLC
Chambersburg PA
CBHW071105120626
46546CB00003B/1280